We Just Love Football

Barry Hindson and Paul Dixon

ISBN 1 901237 25 7

Printed and published by:
TUPS Books, 30 Lime Street,
Newcastle upon Tyne, NE1 2PQ
Tel: 0191 222 0990
Fax: 0191 233 0578

Foreword

by

PETER BEARDSLEY

If you are interested in grass-roots football you will love this book. It captures the passion, humour and dedication of all the people who play, coach and support the game at non-league level.

There have been some fabulous characters on the non-league scene over the years and Barry and Paul have captured their stories. Most of them are hilarious and some of them are very moving.

I still remember playing as a youngster and rubbing shoulders with several of the people in this book and it brings back some great memories. I was lucky and opportunity came my way; others had to settle for playing or coaching careers with their local team. But we all have one thing in common: WE JUST LOVE FOOTBALL.

I am sure you will enjoy reading the great stories and meeting the amazing characters in this book.

Peter Beardsley
November 2001

Contents

STEVE BLACK

Blackie — the Formative Years

Emerging talent

The internationally renowned fitness guru Steve Black's rise to pre-eminence in his chosen career field is well documented elsewhere; the story of his early years, littered as it is with madcap incidents, is less well known beyond the coterie of those with whom he had contact in those crazy days. It takes believing, but every word is true.

The story began at St. Cuthbert's High School in the west end of Newcastle where young Steve first came to prominence as a tricky little outside-right in Stan Eardley's under-twelve side, which played with two orthodox wingers and a big centre-forward and usually won the league. A year later Steve made his debut for Newcastle Boys and he went on to represent the city right through to under-sixteen level:

"I was very tricky, and I got into the Guinness Book of Records because I never passed a ball for three years!"

The strength of mind which has characterised Blackie over the years wasn't long in manifesting itself. He played for Newcastle Boys under Bob Maddison of Kenton School one Saturday and scored a hat-trick, a feat which won him headlines in the local 'Football Pink' as well as public praise from his headmaster in school assembly the following Monday morning:

"We had a school game on the Saturday and when I checked the team sheet I hadn't been picked. I went to see Mr. Knox, the games teacher and told him I wasn't injured and he told me I was conceited for assuming I would be in the side and that he had left me out to keep my feet on the ground. I was 14-years-old and he stopped me playing for the school because I had scored a hat-trick for Newcastle Boys. We get on well enough now but I was strong-minded even then, and I never really played for the school again. They even stopped me playing for Newcastle Boys because I wouldn't play for the school."

Blackie's talent caught the eye of George 'Nobby' Hall who took him for trials at Hull City, where he stayed in digs with another north-east lad a couple of years older than himself called Jimmy McDonald. Steve's sunny disposition made him a favourite with his landlady, who wasn't quite so keen on Jimmy:

"One night we were sitting watching 'Sportsnight' on the telly and she turned to me and asked me if I would like some fish and chips. I said I would love some, then she turned to Jimmy and said 'Mushy peas?' Jimmy nodded

Big brother — little sister

and she went away. When she came back she put this beautiful plate of fish and chips down in front of me and a plate of mushy peas in front of Jimmy."

Incredibly Steve, who to be fair was '13 going on 27' made his footballing debut for Benton Social Club at the age of 13, though he depended on older and more experienced players for protection:

"I was a feisty little character even then and I was going down the wing this Sunday morning beating players on piece. This bloke didn't like it and he tripped me so I jumped up and punched him on the nose. He got up to sort me out but Seppy Ritson came across and flattened him."

He moved from Benton Club to North Heaton Sports Club and at the age of 15 he was brought up before the committee for fighting in the club one Friday night and informed that as a punishment he was to be dropped to the substitute's bench for the upcoming Sunday match against Old Fold Tavern in the semi-finals of the cup:

"I was foaming. Joe Buzzeo, Alan Thompson and 'Rawmeat' Sid Foster were all in the team but they were losing 2-1 and the manager told me to go on and make a difference. I thought 'I'll make a difference all right.' Kevin Matthews came towards me with the ball and I punched him; the referee said, 'I can't believe I saw that — you've only been on the pitch 30 seconds; get off!' The lads were threatening to kill me after the game."

At the same time as he was playing for North Heaton on Sundays Steve was turning out on Saturdays for Andy Kinchley's Parsons works team in the Northern Combination alongside Billy Tarbitt, Billy Small and an ex-Carlisle and Darlington pro called Eric Johnson. Andy Kinchley is remembered by Steve with great affection as his mentor in those early years and 30 years on, with his international reputation in the field of coaching and motivation, he still maintains he has never been with a better football coach; a man who was lost to the top echelons of the game because he was totally engrossed in the local game:

"Andy was running a team in the Northern Combination but he thought he was running Liverpool — and he could have."

Steve moved on from North Heaton to play for Byker St Peter's Middle Club on Sundays and while he was there Billy Todd, the manager of Stanley United, came to watch him and, impressed by the youngster's ability, arranged to meet him in the café of Parrish's department store on Shields Road:

"It was crazy. He wanted me to play for Stanley on Saturdays, so he took me to this café and said I could have anything I wanted to eat and drink. I must say a cup of tea and a scone wasn't the greatest incentive in the world. He told me he wanted me because of my experience; apparently he had a team of 25-year-olds who needed bringing on. I was nearly 17 but when I told him he thought I was a comedian and fell about laughing."

So Stanley lost out and Steve stayed with Parsons, and continued to play with two friends from childhood and kindred spirits: Ian Mutrie and Tommy Hunter in the Newton Park Sunday Team. The team played on the Coach Lane pitches in Newcastle and consisted mainly of young men from Benton and Heaton. They were a very good side but they were a capricious bunch who didn't for one moment take life or football seriously, and some of their antics are the stuff of legend:

"Tommy Hunter, Ian Mutrie and I were partners in crime. I was the team's guest coach and during games I would saunter round the pitch moving the corner flags to make the pitch narrower and narrower. Another time I turned up in an old lumber jacket and I was introduced to the two teams as the Duke of Edinburgh. One of my jobs was to pay the referee, and after one game when he came up to me for his money I asked him if he had any means of identification. He was still wearing his referee's gear and he asked me if I thought he walked about the streets dressed like that. I said we'd had a lot of trouble with blokes dressed as referees trying to con us out of match fees, then I told him men dressed as referees had been seen in the locality swindling old people out of their pension money. He just took his cash and wandered away shaking his head."

Incidentally, one of the players involved with the team was Jimmy Bradford, now known internationally as Jimmy Nail and reckoned by Blackie to be the worst footballer who ever lived but a great singer!

Even Steve will admit that on occasion he took his pranks too far, and he cites an occasion when he was playing for the Middle Club in a cup semi-final. They were losing 2-1 and Steve told his mate Lar Fawcett, (a founder member of the Silly Club with Hunter and Mutrie) who was one of the substitutes, to start up his car and place it beside one of the corner flags with the engine running. The Middle Club won a corner and instead of crossing the ball Steve picked it up, jumped into the car and told Lar to drive away. It was the only ball the team had and the match had to be abandoned. Two weeks later the pair of them turned up at the club with their kit as usual to be told by the doorman that they were in trouble because the club had been charged with bringing the game into disrepute.

"Another time they asked us to pick up three new players and bring them to the game. On the way to the ground we stopped the car, got a groundsheet out of the boot, laid it at the side of the road. Then Lar and me got our papers out and sat on the groundsheet reading them until after kick-off time. The three lads hadn't a clue what was going on, and we couldn't wait to tell Ian Mutrie and Tommy so that we could get one up on them in the crazy stakes. That was at Wallsend Athletic, lovingly run by Cyril Marr."

Steve was still only 16, and as well as training as an accountant he was working as a doorman at the city nightspots and holding down a variety of part-time jobs. In addition he had signed amateur forms with Newcastle United, with whom he trained at Hunters Moor alongside players like Colin Chambers and Paul Cannell:

"I had all these jobs and I was making fortunes, but I was a good spender as well. We trained at Hunters Moor but I don't think the coach liked me very much because of my ways. He told me to do press-ups once and I couldn't do them because I had a plaster cast on my arm, and shortly after that they told me I could go to Darlington or Hartlepool. I told them to go to

Looking a shade fit with his Nan and sister Ros

hell. It was a pity because I had outstanding ability. I could keep the ball in the air over 3000 times and I had such a high skill level I could decide to play a whole game using just one foot. I had never been known to pass the ball but I decided to give it a try and I was sensational, but it was too easy. What I really needed at that time in my life was proper mature guidance but there was no-one to provide it. I had so many things going on in my life and to be honest, being the toughest kid in the town was as high a priority as being the best footballer."

After the experience of being released by Newcastle United and being advised to pursue his football career at a lower level, Steve gave up playing and took his first steps on the coaching ladder while continuing to work the doors in town. At the age of 18 he began to watch Byker Legion play on Sunday mornings and it was at this time that he became friendly with another two kindred spirits in Dave Short and Micky Cogan. Although he wasn't playing his involvement was such that he was always included in Byker Legion's end-of-season celebrations, often to devastating effect.

Sunday League end-of-season presentations were normally held in the Mayfair Ballroom, a massive venue in the centre of Newcastle. One occasion saw Byker Legion on hand to receive the trophies as both league champions and cup winners, but the first award of the evening was presented to the season's most sporting team. The recipients were Maccabi FC, the local Jewish club which rarely if ever won a game but invariably behaved with impeccable sportsmanship. The award was announced by league officials Charlie Taylor and Lennie Cheetham, whereupon Steve, who is dark of complexion and was sporting long black hair as well as his trademark black beard, decided to intervene:

"I stepped into the spotlight and walked through the massed ranks up onto the stage and collected the trophy. I lifted it up for the audience to see, took a bow and as they clapped and cheered I walked off the stage with the cup, chased by the manager of Maccabi, who had his acceptance speech in his hand and was screaming, 'Where are you going with our trophy?'"

On another infamous occasion an end-of-season fancy-dress party was organised at the Lord Clyde pub near Cramlington. A double-decker bus was hired to pick everyone up and transport them to the function, but when they made a stop at one of the pre-arranged locations on Benton Road to collect one of the players there was nobody to be seen except an eccentric window-cleaner cleaning the windows of one of the houses in a manner more than a little reminiscent of Norman Wisdom. It turned out to be Dave Short, who eventually got on the bus with his bucket and wash-leather to join the party. The next port of call was the Rocket pub in Longbenton, where Billy Petford was waiting. Billy was a real character and a lover of the opposite sex who pretended to be a dancer and only spoke French when he went into town on Saturday nights. He had decided to go to the party dressed as a woman, which broke his mother's heart because in spite of his reputation as a ladies' man she had always harboured doubts about his orientation, and when he appeared dressed as a woman her worst fears appeared to be confirmed. Billy wasn't lacking in courage either:

"The Rocket is a pub where you can get a pint, a pie and a fight, not necessarily in that order, and when we got there Billy was sitting in the bar dressed as a woman and reading his paper."

On they went to Killingworth where to their surprise a lollipop man stopped the bus despite the fact that it was seven o'clock at night and there wasn't a child in sight. One of the players, Micky Cogan, had no fancy dress and when he was stopped by a lollipop man that afternoon he offered the man ten pounds to borrow his stick and uniform for the party!

Eventually the bus arrived at the Lord Clyde and Steve Black and Dave Short were the first two to disembark. The disco was warming up, the function room was beautiful and a sumptuous buffet lovingly prepared by the landlord's wife was the centre piece:

"I spotted this lovely strawberry gateau on the buffet so I picked it up and pushed it straight into Shortie's face, so he did the same to me with the chocolate gateau. In seconds there was food everywhere. The manager was distraught and Andy Kinchley was trying to placate him but he was dressed as a schoolgirl, which didn't help. John Wilson who ran the team with Andy was walking up and down the street saying it was the worst night of his life. Then Billy Petford pretended to pinch cutlery and hide it in his handbag. By now the landlord was having a nervous breakdown and his wife was in hysterics. Then came little Joe Young who had come in a yellow oilskin and sou'wester like Captain Birdseye. He burst into the room and shouted 'Tarran!' so everybody threw their beer over him. It was absolute mayhem and it was only 20 to eight; we'd only been there ten minutes. Anyway, things settled down after that; we helped to clean up and we spent loads of money so we had a great night and the landlord was happier when he counted his takings."

There were further high jinks to come on the journey home. Micky Quinn had borrowed a fur stole from Ian Playfair's wife to go to the party as a caveman and the players took it off him and threw him off the bus in the middle of nowhere, stark naked:

"The last I heard he was wandering along the motorway bollock-naked and in tears."

The first senior team Steve Black coached, along with Bob Momon, was the Black Bull pub side in Benton. He took over from Jimmy McCarthy and although the team was in the 'B' division of the North East Sunday League it might just as well have been Barcelona, it was so important to him. His two assistants were Joe and Ned McLean:

"Ned knew loads of swear-words and he made the soup, and Joe had a long overcoat like John Motson so he was management. Joe had signed a pledge never to smile, and Ned was the opposite of me; I was totally positive but he would just tell the players they were absolute shite of the highest order."

Steve was developing his coaching skills, but his bizarre lifestyle still manifested itself both with himself and his players; he told Billy Dodds to cover as much ground as possible so he lay on the pitch and spread his arms and legs as wide as he could. Another of his players was Michael Rickards, a six-feet-six beanpole:

"He was the best kicker-in before a game ever, and he thought he was brilliant. I made it known that what the team needed to take it to the next level of success was a top-class keeper and I promised to produce the best, but I wouldn't reveal his identity beyond saying he was known as 'The Cat.' It was the talk of all the bars in Benton and on the Sunday this massive crowd turned up to see who he was. The players were in the changing room and the door was kicked open and there stood Rickards with new gloves yelling 'The return of the cat'. He wore these white plimsolls and we were 9-0 down by half time; he was complaining that he needed more protection."

They were quite a bunch of characters; one of the players was a favourite with the ladies and would often emerge from the bushes in his playing kit and run onto the pitch while his girlfriend followed him in a state of disarray, promising to see him later. The other side of the coin, however, was that they were a highly talented bunch of footballers and when people like Frankie Law, Davie Woodhouse, Billy Dodds and Roy Collins put their minds to it they were capable of playing any side off the pitch. Craziness, though, was the predominant factor:

Cooking up a session

"We had a man-of-the-match award every Sunday after the game in the Black Bull. It would be something like a tin of pease pudding or a toddler's reading book. Once it was an all-expenses-paid trip to the terminus and back on the number 37 bus. I got the manager-of-the-month award, a bottle of whisky, every week, and at the end of season 'do' we had this rule that they could drink anything they wanted as long as it was Best Scotch."

They signed a player who had been in the Royal Air Force and at half-time on his debut he came into the dressing-room where Blackie had laid out the post-match buffet with sandwiches, cakes and jelly and custard. The player asked for a drink of water and that was sufficient to make him their next victim. Pressed to have something to eat he said he didn't like the idea of eating food half-way through a game. 'You shithouse,' he was told, 'Blackie's mother's been up all night making that food.' Shamed into eating, he consumed several sandwiches and a plate of jelly and custard, as a consequence of which he came off in the second half feeling sick and unable to run. He left and never returned.

Another victim was Ronnie Walker: he had been a good player but a lifestyle inspired by smoking and drinking had taken a heavy toll on his physical condition. He was persuaded to play one Sunday morning, and in the days leading up to the game Blackie went through his familiar routine of building up the mystique surrounding his new signing. When the game kicked off Ronnie took one stride and pulled both a stomach and a calf muscle. The level of hilarity this produced was such that no-one was capable of helping him.

At the same time as he was involved with his Sunday team Steve was running a Saturday team out of the Innisfree Catholic Club in the Tyneside

Amateur League with many of the same players, assisted on the administrative side by the father-and-son team of Percy and Alan Turner:

"We were crazy, but the coaching was innovative and that was where my ideas evolved. The team talks had more depth and substance than you get in the Premiership. Some of them lasted an hour, which was ridiculous, but if it had been a coaching video it would have been sensational. I tried to get the players time off work on the basis that if they were playing at three o'clock they should train at three o'clock. I was asking myself questions all the time although people didn't necessarily take it seriously because it was so different. I was so crazy in other aspects of my life that I couldn't expect to be taken seriously."

He was serious, though, and in 1999 when the Welsh national rugby XV which he coached defeated England at Wembley 32-31 and he was asked by the massed media at the post-match press conference if he had ever experienced comparable feelings of elation and satisfaction he replied that the only other such occasion had been when the Innisfree beat DSS 2-1 in the Tyneside Amateur League.

Steve Black continued to cause consternation, uproar and hilarity in abundance. There was the occasion at a football talk-in when he spent ten minutes formulating a question for the then manager of Southampton Lawrie McMenemy, commenting on the impressive nature of the team's appearance when they took the field in their immaculate kit, the flow of their bodies in their silky shorts, the quality of his players such as Kevin Keegan, Alan Ball and Mick Channon, and how it contrasted with his own team's ragged appearance when they took the field. Eventually, with the entire audience in hysterics, he came to

his question; which detergent did Southampton use to wash their kit?

On a similar occasion he deliberately confused the star guest, the dour manager of Newcastle United, Bill McGarry, with a flamboyant and extrovert former Newcastle player called Ron McGarry:

"I told him I remembered him as a player and that he had been a great goal-scorer and how inspired it was when he nicknamed himself Cassius after he was red-carded for punching an opponent. I went on about the business cards he had printed with 'Have Goals Will Travel' on them. I gave him all this nonsense then asked him how the present Newcastle team compared with the promotion side in which he had played. Bob Cass was the chairman and when he said he thought I was confusing Bill with Ron I pretended to be embarrassed and apologetic — the place was in hysterics."

The formative years of Steve Black almost defy belief, but what is certain is that from those crazy capers emerged a coach of world renown who worked with Kevin Keegan in his magical years as manager of Newcastle United, with Glenn McCrory when he became world boxing champion, with the most successful Welsh rugby union side of all time, and with his present employer Rob Andrew when the Newcastle Falcons won the inaugural Allied Dunbar Premiership title. His reputation as a coach is a worldwide one based on vision and innovation:

"I had to get a different perspective. People asked me to do sessions because they were lazy and at first they thought that maybe I'd have novelty value, but when I joined in the five-a-sides and they realised I could play I gradually won their respect, as did the fact that their winning percentages invariably became more positive. I was able to see things clearly and with a fresh eye in all sports. Other coaches did it the way they had been coached and when they saw me doing something different they wondered where I got it from, and my credibility grew. But I'd travelled all over the world observing and learning until I became a properly rounded practitioner with a unique approach which invariably brought with it success."

Steve Black's star continues to ascend; appointed coach to the British Lions for the 2001 tour of Australia — there is probably a not a higher coaching accolade in the Northern hemisphere. He has rejuvenated a fading Newcastle Falcons team since he returned from Wales and has taken Sunderland Football Club to the brink of European qualification. His impact as an innovative coach on the world of sport is beyond our brief. Our task has been to catalogue some of the incidents from his previous existence which have helped to mould a unique and gifted character; and with Blackie they really did break the mould.

Receiving his award at the Sports Council Dinner at Newcastle Civic Centre

British Lions Tour 2001 — Steve with Jason Robinson

TONY CASSIDY

The goalkeeper who cried but went to Wembley.

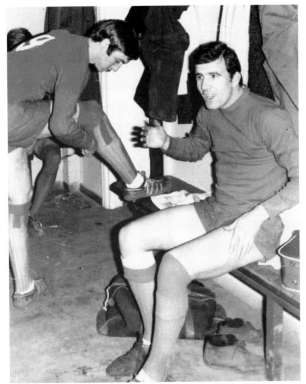

Getting ready for action at North Shields

Tony Cassidy's football career began when he was selected for the Central Junior School in Wallsend against Carville School; a game his school lost 2-0:

"I had always wanted to be a goalkeeper but I let two in that day. One of them went through my legs and when I got home I cried. I told my mother I would never play in goal again and I never have. Not even in training."

His goalkeeping days may have been short-lived but his career in football was to be a long and distinguished one. The next steps were a change of school and a change of position which saw him playing for the Stephenson Memorial School as an attacking full-back in a team which twice won the prestigious Blake Cup.

At the age of 15 Tony left school and was due to start work in the Swan Hunter shipyard. In his spare time he would go with his pal Malcolm Peel, who was a goalkeeper, to practise their skills in the Swan Hunter playing field. One night he was approached by Jackie Miller (whose son Keith is now a respected player) and invited to play that weekend for Swan Hunters Reserves against their first team:

> "They had this big hard lad playing for them but as I passed him I laid him out. I scored a goal as well and they asked me to sign for them. Malcolm wasn't asked because they already had an excellent keeper called Tex Holmes."

Tony played for Swan Hunters first team at right-half the following week against Wallsend Corinthians — who had an excellent side including Ronnie Jarvis, Stevie Jackson and Eric Hunter — and the Corinthians won 13-1; Tony's minor consolation was scoring the goal, and afterwards he joined Corinthians to play in their junior side under the guidance of Stan Hitchens. It was a good side laden with talented players like Norman Dunn, Norman Gall, Geordie Little and Davie Burns, and one of the coaches was the Sunderland scout Charlie Ferguson:

> "Charlie asked me if I would go to Sunderland but I was a West Brom fan; I loved their strip and I was a great admirer of players like Ray Barlow and Ronnie Allen. I still sign domino cards 'WBA' but West Brom never came in for me. Newcastle were also interested and I was torn between the two North-East camps."

By now the sixteen-year-old Tony Cassidy was captaining Wallsend Corinthians and his confidence in his own ability was sky high. When he told his father he was as good as Denis Law but hadn't had the same lucky breaks it may have had the whiff of youthful conceit, but Tony believed it. His senior career destination was finally decided when Bob Keen, the Secretary of Gateshead, came to his parents' house and asked him to sign. He agreed to go to Gateshead and he signed for them despite the fact that they lost their league status to Peterborough United at the end of that season:

> "Jack Fairbrother, the old Newcastle goalkeeper, was Gateshead's manager and Norman Hunter was there as a young player. In my first-team debut we beat Wigan 2-1 in the FA Cup. I was an amateur then and listening to the professionals at half-time in that cup-tie I realised what the pro game was about and how serious it was. I was in a new world and I knew I had to learn fast. I was physically strong but emotionally there were others who were more mature."

That Gateshead side was a useful one; the legendary Johnny Ingham was still playing outside-right and they included Rod Cameron, Joe Armstrong and Alan Burridge in their line-up. The games were covered for the local paper by a young reporter called John Gibson, who is now the club chairman! Sadly, Jack Fairbrother's wife died in tragic circumstances, and Charlie Ferguson took over as manager. Ferguson was still keen to take Tony to Sunderland but the lad knew in his heart that he wasn't quite good enough:

> "I had a great engine and I could run for hours, and I had confidence in my ability, but I knew I didn't have that initial burst of pace to take me away from players; I wasn't quite sharp enough."

In those days there was an odd number of teams in the Scottish Second Division and Gateshead travelled up north each Friday night to play whichever team had a blank Saturday. The club had ambitions to play in the Scottish league and their application was treated sympathetically; in anticipation of their acceptance they resigned from the North-Eastern League, but their application was turned down in the end and they joined the North Regional League:

"I played two games every weekend. I once scored a hat-trick at Falkirk on the Friday night and two against North Shields at Appleby Park on the Saturday. After the Falkirk game they took me into the boardroom and asked me to sign but big George Aitken, who always looked after me, stormed in from the shower bollock-naked and chased me out. He gave Charlie Ferguson a right telling-off."

Lawrie McMenemy came to Gateshead to coach the reserve team and although his stay was a short one before he went into management he won the respect of Tony Cassidy. Gateshead sent Tony to a range of clubs for trials in the hopes of raising revenue from any potential transfer, and one of his ports of call was Preston, where he remembers Tommy Docherty complaining that while all the players received £12 a week in the playing season he was only paid £10 in the summer while Tom Finney received £12. He was told the reason was that Finney was a better player than him, to which Docherty replied with one of his immortal lines: "Not in the summer he isn't."

Tony decided his time had run out at Gateshead and he found himself becoming disenchanted with the management style of Ferguson's successor, another Newcastle favourite, Bobby Mitchell, and he elected to move on. He was playing Sunday morning football for Buists the car distributors,

and he played a game against the Birds Nest at Harbottle Park:

"We had an excellent side. Keith Wanless, Bobby Elwell, Ronnie Jarvis and Davie Burns all played and we beat the Birds Nest 4-1, which was a massive upset."

Kenny Walshaw, the manager of North Shields, was at the game and he told Tony his club were going into the Northern League as an amateur side in the following 1962 season. Tony signed for them, and stayed 12 years. Walshaw signed Joe Gidney, Micky Mahon, Micky Lister and Stafford Newham to form the nucleus of a good side, and Tony had the distinction of scoring the first goal for North Shields as an amateur club:

"We beat West Auckland 7-0 and Brian Joicey scored six. After the game he complained that he couldn't win. He had scored six but everyone was talking about the screamer I scored."

Kenny Walshaw continued to recruit quality players. Don Winskill came in and scored 67 goals in a season, and John Twaddle, Bomber Thompson and Ronnie Tatum were added to the squad. The local 'Tyne Brand' food company had a factory in Holland and through them a tour was arranged which included a match against Haarlem, who were enthusing about a ten-year-old kid in their junior ranks; his name was Ruud Gullit.

Tony and Ronnie Tatum were close friends and the other players would bring their grievances to them; on the Dutch trip it was the manager's turn to express his concerns. Frank Brennan had come on the tour as a guest and Kenny felt it was the prelude to the former Newcastle centre-half taking over the management of the team:

"Kenny wasn't a drinker but we got him drunk, dressed him up in Dutch national costume and

North Shields FC with the Amateur Cup in 1969

he ended up singing 'Pennies from Heaven', but it was his swansong. They bombed him out and Brennan took over a ready-made side."

Tony was playing inside-left for Shields, so when Brennan signed the Whitley Bay number ten Ray Wrightson he thought his place was in jeopardy. Coincidentally he had an opportunity to join Queen of the South, but Brennan reassured him that he had signed Wrightson to play as a winger and that his place was secure. He was also

informed by the chairman that the club wanted him to stay, so he remained at Appleby Park. It was a fateful decision, because had he followed his initial instinct and gone to Scotland he would have missed out on the following season when North Shields won the FA Amateur Cup!

There was a belief in the team that 1969 could be North Shields' year, and when they overcame a potentially difficult first-round hurdle against Spennymoor relatively easily the belief was reinforced. A comfortable win over Oswestry was followed by a home tie against Walthamstow Avenue:

"There was a clash in the penalty area; their keeper was sent off and we got a penalty. Our regular penalty-taker, Micky Lister, wasn't playing so Bomber Thompson took the kick. He hit it so hard and high over the bar that we never got the ball back, but Richie Hall scored a late winner."

Shields were drawn at home to Hendon in the next round — an outstanding amateur side whose goalkeeper John Swannell had won over 100 England caps. There was a big crowd and a tremendous atmosphere at Appleby Park for the tie, which Shields drew thanks to a late Ray Wrightson equaliser. The team travelled to London for the replay the following Friday, but when they woke up on the Saturday morning they found the pitch frozen, and the game was postponed for a week:

"I had a day when God decided that everything I did would come off. We won 2-0 and Brian Joicey scored both the goals from my passes. We were in the semi-finals of the Amateur Cup and people told me I would be picked for England because the manager had been at the match. I knew different though, because the England captain played in my position."

Confirmation of Tony's outstanding contribution to that victory came on the BBC's 'Sports Report' that night when their reporter declared that Hendon 'had no answer to John Rutherford and Tony Cassidy on the North Shields left.'

The semi-finals threw up the possibility of an all-north-east final with Shields drawn against Skelmersdale at Middlesbrough and Whitley Bay against Sutton United at Birmingham. Certainly all the neutrals in the area hoped that would be the outcome, but the North Shields players wanted Whitley to lose so that they could have all the glory! The match against Skelmersdale was played in a quagmire at Ayresome Park and Shields went a goal down when Micky Burns, later of Newcastle United, put their opponents in front. Worse was to follow when Alan Driver was sent off late in the first half. Brennan rearranged his side, taking Ray Wrightson off, moving Micky Lister to right-back and bringing on Tommy Orrick. The strategy worked when Tony rolled a pass to Micky Lister to run on to and cross to the far post where Orrick was on hand to score the equaliser and earn a replay at Stockport.

At the Thursday night training session before the replay Brennan introduced a new element into the North Shields armoury by concentrating on 'professional' fouls and instructing his players that he wanted them to adopt a physical approach. Micky Burns again gave Skelmersdale the lead but they were knocked out of their stride by the more robust tactics of North Shields, and when Brian Joicey equalised there was only going to be one winner. They won a left-wing corner which was headed clear to Tony, who lobbed it back into the danger area for Joicey to score the decisive goal:

"We couldn't believe we were in the final at Wembley and we were elated but when we passed their dressing room and saw how dejected they were we realised it could have been us and that put a temporary dampener on our euphoria."

Chairman Maurice Merrick arranged for the team bus to stop at the Eden Arms at Rushyford in County Durham on the way back, and a wonderful night of celebrations ensued. The North Shields team were worthy of their place at Wembley. They had a sound keeper, two solid full-backs; Ronnie Tatum was a great tackler and Bomber Thompson played with his heart on his sleeve, and they were a superb centre-back pairing, Tony shared midfield responsibilities with Dickie Hall, a Quaker from Penshaw, and up front they had a brilliant finisher in Brian Joicey. The wingers, John Rutherford and Ray Wrightson, were both accomplished dribblers and crossers, and Micky Lister's role was to sit in behind Joicey and glide into dangerous situations. It was a very capable and well-balanced side.

The build-up to the final was magnificently handled by Frank Brennan, who deflected all the media attention so that his players could focus on their preparations for the match. At the Tuesday night training session in cup-final week there were a number of representatives from boot manufacturers in attendance, inviting players to wear their products in the final:

"I chose a pair of Puma boots. I had this belief that every time I wore new boots I played well. We travelled on Friday 10th April and I have to say that when we went to Wembley for a look around I was disappointed. I said it looked like a cabbage patch and I was quoted in the 'Newcastle Journal' the next day. I was just disappointed because I was expecting it to be sacred turf."

The players were taken to the Victoria Palace theatre to see the 'Black and White Minstrel Show' and afterwards at the hotel Brennan instructed his players to replicate their normal Friday night habits but to be in bed by 11.30pm. A couple of pints was the norm and it was a relaxed group of players who went off to bed that night, with a couple of exceptions:

"I roomed with Bomber Thompson and we couldn't sleep. I tried to teach him how to play chess; it was a complete waste of time but it relaxed me and I got a decent sleep."

Next morning Frank took his players to Hyde Park for a gentle warm-up, then back to the hotel for a shower followed by a late breakfast of steak and scrambled eggs. He then outlined his game plan, and the team coach set off for Wembley. The Wembley dressing rooms are huge — Micky Morgan reckoned it was possible to swim a length in the team bath — and after the preliminaries the players made their way down the tunnel and onto the pitch:

"This time it was the real Wembley. It seemed to have been transformed. We spotted our wives in the stand straight away and that helped us to relax. We were introduced to the Marquis of Blandford but I couldn't wait to get down to our end and smack a practice shot into the back of the net."

When the game kicked off Frank Brennan went down the tunnel to change into his track suit and when he returned a couple of minutes later his team was a goal down! They got back into the game, but there was a defining moment just before half time when Sutton were awarded a free kick from which they created an excellent goalscoring opportunity. However, they missed from two yards out and instead of being dead and buried Shields were reprieved to the extent that they were only a goal down at the break:

"At half-time Frank told Dickie Hall and me to slow down, look around and just go where we had to go. We took his advice and we began to take over. Tommy Orrick came on for Ray Wrightson and when we got a corner Dickie Hall scored the equaliser at the far post. I went to congratulate him but all the other players turned to Sutton and told them they were beaten. Then

Old Boys' reunion night

Brian Joicey stumbled through two tackles to put us in front. We were in control and in the last minute John Rutherford and I were passing the ball between us in the corner and singing the North Shields anthem 'Everybody wants to go to heaven but nobody wants to die.' When the final whistle went I was so pleased for my team-mates and the fans. The support on the terraces was fantastic; they were a mass of red and white. There were 47,000 at that game and I've met all 94,000 of them since!"

Tony and his team-mates were surprised to see one of the Sutton players leaving the pitch during the playing of the National Anthem after the game, but it transpired that he had just played in his fifth losing final!

After the game Frank Brennan, not normally a man noted for his generosity, took the players to his hotel room and provided champagne, whisky and cigars as he explained what it meant to him to have won at Wembley both as a player and a manager. That night there was a reception for the victorious team at their Clifton Ford Hotel, and during the celebrations Tony was paged over the tannoy to go to reception:

"When I got there my parents were waiting to see me. My father said; 'Son, I'm so proud of you.' It was very emotional and it was a big day. The chairman invited them to the function but they said it was my day and they wouldn't stay."

The Amateur Cup winners came home by train the following day and the club secretary Charlie Munro informed them that there was an open-topped bus waiting to take them from Newcastle Central Station to North Shields. The players were expecting to go home by taxi and only agreed with some reluctance to go on the bus, believing no-one would turn out to greet them:

"It was incredible. You couldn't see the station for people and the police had to get us through the crowds to the bus. There were people on every street in Newcastle and as we drove through Brennan gave the cup to Bomber Thompson because he was a Newcastle lad. In Byker they gave it to Tommy Orrick and when we got to Wallsend they gave it to me because I was from there. The streets were thronged and by the time we got to Percy Main the bus could only crawl. When we turned into Northumberland Square in North Shields it was impossible to move for people. The mayor was waiting to give us a champagne reception, then we went onto the Town Hall balcony and there was just a sea of people below. After that it was back to the football club for more backslapping and handshaking, then onto the pitch for a photograph. That photo was hung behind the clubhouse bar and when the place was pulled down Keith Houghton told me it was in a bin, so I went round and rescued it and now it's in my garage."

The days that followed were hectic; there were still 13 games to play, and everywhere North Shields played there was a reception for the team. Incredibly they won 12 and drew one of those games, and a 4-1 win on the last day of the season (despite a Tony Cassidy own goal) saw them pip their old rivals Whitley Bay for the league championship to add to the league cup, the Northumberland Senior Cup and, of course, the FA Amateur Cup. More glamour followed when they played for the European Amateur Cup in the Olympic Stadium in Rome: the match was drawn and it was agreed that Shields would take the winners' medals and their opponents would keep the trophy. It had been quite a season.

Tony Cassidy spent 12 years at North Shields before he left following a disagreement with Frank Brennan:

"I didn't bare him any grudges though, and the way he orchestrated things at Wembley that day we won the Amateur Cup was fabulous. My only regret is that when he died I was the only one of the team at his funeral. That's sad."

A brief spell at Durham City before returning to North Shields preceded a new chapter in Tony's career. He had taken his coaching badges and he became player/manager at Marine Park in the Northern Alliance, where his team included Bobby Lodge, George Stoneham, Billy Allen, Micky Barry, the Colwill brothers and Richard Percy:

"My ambition was always to win the Northumberland Senior Cup with Marine Park, but the nearest we got was losing a semi-final replay at Whitley Bay against the run of play. That was my biggest disappointment but I can claim to have been an innovative coach. I was analysing games like Andy Gray does now and I learned from people like Malcolm Allison and Don Revie, mixing in my own ideas. For instance, at Leeds they played five-a-sides for an apple

Happy days at Marine Park FC

each and I did the same at Marine Park for pints of beer."

Tony enjoyed coaching, seeking to reduce players' faults and increase their competitive edge, and in three seasons he won three league championships and three league cups, the latter at St James' Park. The people who ran Marine Park, however, didn't share his ambition to take the club higher, so he took his players with him to South Shields, where they twice finished runners-up in the Wearside League.

So to the final phase of a remarkably successful career in non-league football. Tony was 39 when he was approached by Chief Inspector John Weirs, an ex-goalkeeper whose appetite for the game was as huge as his six-feet-six frame. John was forming an over-40 side to play friendlies and he had no difficulty in persuading Tony to play. The following season they joined a Sunderland-based league where initially the standard wasn't high, but very soon old professionals and Northern League players took up the idea and standards rose rapidly:

"It extended my career by seven or eight years and I thoroughly enjoyed playing for Marden. I

Tony and his wife, Joan

got some of the old lads together and it was a case of 40 minutes each way followed by food and drink provided for the away team by the home team and a lot of 'all our yesterdays'. The standards of play, pitches and refereeing have all risen and we have people who would rather watch us on a Saturday morning than go to a game in the afternoon."

After a while John Weirs reduced his up-front involvement, though he continued to work behind the scenes, and Tony took over, first as player/manager then running the team:

"Atmosphere was everything at Marine Park and when I brought those same players to Marden it was the same. We won everything on offer and we have maintained the highest standards for

18 years. I would still be doing it now if it wasn't for my work commitments, but things are in safe hands because Richard Percy has taken over."

Tony Cassidy has always believed in the hand of fate and he doesn't regret the few mistakes he has made, perhaps most significantly when he turned down the post of coach to Newcastle United juniors in the Gordon Lee era:

"I had a wife and three kids and a job in the shipyards. I couldn't have managed on the money and if I hadn't been a success I would have been in limbo. I would rather have gone to work in a track suit than a boiler suit but I've got no regrets. The game has been good to me: I've met some wonderful people and been to some great places. It's a beautiful game."

BILLY CAWTHRA

George Best, a hatpin and victory at Wembley

Northumberland Football Association
Football Association Counties Youth Champions 1968-1969

Billy Cawthra, who throughout his long career built a well-deserved reputation as an outstanding goalscorer, first attracted attention as a goalkeeper! As a 15-year-old pupil at Gosforth High School in Newcastle he played in goal for South Northumberland Boys until the occasion when his side was beaten 7-1 by Newcastle Boys:

> "It was like the Alamo and I thought 'get me out of here.' The teacher thought the same."

The claims of older boys made it hard for Billy to break into the school team as an outfield player until one day there was a call from his sports master 'Punchy' Bates, a well-known club rugby player who brooked no denial. Mr. Bates told him he was selected to play centre-forward for the school that night:

> "I had no boots and even at that age I had size-11 feet, but like all schools we had a fat lad with

glasses and an ancient pair of boots. I borrowed those, we beat Seaton Burn High School 6-1 and I scored five. I was a natural goal-scorer."

In his last year at school he played centre-forward in a South Northumberland side which included Ray Kennedy — who was to enjoy a fabulous career with Arsenal, Liverpool and England. At that stage young Ray was a small, quiet lad but he blossomed into an outstanding player.

When Billy left school he started work as an apprentice plumber and began his boys' club career with Montague and North Fenham:

> "I didn't know there were such things as boys' clubs. We didn't have anything like that in Gosforth, but Montagu was one of the best. I played with lads like Paddy Lowery, Dave Huck, who was a prolific goalscorer, and Dixie Armstrong. The team was run by 'Big' Dick Almond who was over 20 stones. When he came to our house to sign me my mother thought she would get a new settee out of it he was so big. The club was so well run; they had sponsors 30 years ago. We won the league and cup both years I was there and our main rivals were St. Mary's who had players like Brian Spells and Micky Spellman."

On one occasion five of the Montagu team were selected to represent the county in a match at Brighton on the south coast. On the journey down they played cards to pass the time, and being of an age when they were beginning to be aware of the attractions of beer as well as girls, they agreed that whoever won the £5 pot would buy the beer; it cost £10!

Having arrived safely in Brighton they were in the dressing-room listening to the team talk when the door opened and Billy's dad, Bill Cawthra senior, popped in to wish them good luck. Mr.

Cawthra worked on the railways and he happened to have made the journey to Brighton that day:

> "My dad was very supportive, but in a quiet and undemonstrative way. Quite often I didn't know he was there but afterwards he would tell my mother how I had played."

During his last season at Montagu and North Fenham boys' club Billy was approached by a player called 'Curly' Elliott after playing in a cup final and asked to play for Coxlodge Legion in the Sunday League the next day:

> "I lived half a mile away and I didn't know they had a team. Anyway, I turned up and these men were passing me on their way into the dressing room and saying 'hello Bobby.' Then Curly came and he said to the manager 'this is the lad I told you about.' 'Okay son, you're in goal,' he said. I was flabbergasted. I'd played centre-forward in a cup final the day before and now I was a goalkeeper again.

> "In the dressing room afterwards I told Curly my name was Billy. 'Jesus,' he said, 'You're the centre forward. I thought you were Bobby Thompson the goalie!' I played two more games in goal and Billy Howard the manager said I was the best goalkeeper they'd had all season."

The Coxlodge Legion side was a young one, but it matured and gelled quickly with the likes of Alan Wilson and Bobby Kettle in the ranks. They also included a coloured lad called Harry Powell:

> "The culture was different then. He had great talent and he would have been a pro today. One day at North Shields I took my girlfriend to the match. She was standing outside the dressing room and one of the lads asked who the smart blonde was. Harry, who was bollock naked, went out to have a look. He was a very well endowed lad and she had a different attitude to me after that."

The successful Coxlodge Legion Sunday Team

The Coxlodge team developed and improved. Wilf Waite who worked at the Department of Social Security complex at Longbenton strengthened the squad by recruiting players from there — the likes of Billy Blair, Jimmy Henderson, Richard Percy and Stan Bishop — and although they were almost all 18 or 19 they were taking on the best Sunday Morning sides like Newcastle Black Bull and Byker Legion in cup competitions and beating them. In two seasons they won the two major Sunday Morning cups:

"They were a great team and I've got great affection for them. They were all lads from Kenton, Fawdon and Gosforth and they all became top players at local level. Unfortunately the Social club was struggling to back us and the team broke up. I went to play for the Runnymede under Billy Redhead."

On Saturdays Billy had been playing at a good level for the Department of Social Security in the Northern Combination before joining Heaton Stannington, who were run by Lou Henry and Tommy Boylan:

"Heaton Stann had a great coach in Lou Henry and players like Paul Jackson who was a fabulous winger but he wasn't really bothered. They had Dave Short who was a very good centre-half and Barry King who was an outstanding goalscorer. Peter Stephenson played on the left wing; great player. I was only there a season but it was an education. They made us all shareholders to encourage loyalty, then the director promised a free night on the drink if we surrendered our shares. We drank the place dry and the directors were later taken to court by the trustees for trying to sell the ground for a supermarket."

From Heaton Stannington Billy was approached by Jackie Marks to go to Ashington. Bobby Elwell was also keen for him to sign for North Shields and even suggested that he could play for Ashington in the league and North Shields in the cup competitions. Ashington won the day.

"Ashington was a massive club but it had lost its supporter base. Jimmy Henderson told me that. Jimmy was a great friend; Charlie Ferguson took him to Sunderland when he was 15 and he played in the reserves with Charlie Hurley and George Herd. Jimmy was playing left-back and the winger left him for dead a couple of times, then Hurley told him if he didn't put him in the seats next time he'd kick his arse."

Jimmy Henderson had the ability to become a successful professional footballer but when he went back to play for Montague and North Fenham Dick Almond picked him up by the legs, proclaiming 'we've got a star.' Unfortunately he dropped Jimmy, who fell awkwardly and broke his knees; an injury which confined his future career to non-league level.

"Ashington was a learning curve and Jackie Marks was a one-off. The club sponsor was an estate agent and he hadn't a clue about playing but he used to train with us and he loved it. Vin Pearson and Les Mutrie were in the team and the keeper was Eddie Nesbitt; he was six feet tall and nearly as wide. Malcolm Macdonald was playing for Newcastle at the time and he and his wife did our end-of-season presentation.

They sat at our table and we all got our rounds in —I was second last as usual. Eventually Supermac said, 'I'll see you lads' and Eddie Nesbitt said, 'You'll see no bugger 'til you've been to that bar and got the beers in.' And he did"

Life at Ashington was seldom dull and free from incident and on one fairly typical occasion there was a fracas in the tunnel at Durham City after the game:

"There was a bit of argy-bargy and Jimmy Henderson got a hold of Ray Wilkie's brother. He bent him over and kicked him up the arse, propelling him across the dressing room so that he ended up in the team bath."

Billy was at Ashington for a season but he wasn't able to hold down a regular place in the team. He and fellow striker Les Mutrie had been left out for one particular game in favour of a striker who had just been released by Everton, and they were having a drink in the clubhouse when it was discovered that the ex-Everton man wasn't eligible, so Billy was drafted in. He played but it was clearly an unsatisfactory situation and he left to finish the season with Stanley United before returning to Heaton Stannington in the Wearside League:

"We were playing at Marine Park one day and as we were walking out onto the pitch I noticed a horse tethered at the bottom of the field. Billy Colwill was playing for them and he spotted some horse-shit on the grass. He turned to one of their players and said 'How did this shit get on the pitch?'

"'I don't know Billy,' came the reply, 'I didn't pick the team.'"

For two years Billy Cawthra played for Heaton Stannington on Saturdays and Byker Legion on

Sundays. The Legion had a tremendous team run by Andy Kinchley, a quiet character who contrasted with his co-manager John Wilson;

"John was a monster and they had a 'good cop, bad cop' routine which worked perfectly. Once we were playing at Felling on a pitch right alongside the by-pass. Dave Short complained of feeling ill and during the game Jimmy Henderson, who was playing sweeper, shouted 'Everybody out' to his defence to try and catch the opposition offside, but this little voice said 'I cannot Jimmy.' It was Dave Short and he was having a shite on the pitch. At our home ground we changed in a hut with no lights and it was pitch black. The strips didn't always get washed and the next week Kenny Webster, who was just a youngster, wore the same shirt Dave Short had used to wipe his arse at Felling. Nobody told him and he played the whole game in this shirt with shite all down the back."

Byker Legion retained their name although they were based in different locations at times, including one season when they played out of Benton Social Club. This was the era when strippers were the standard Sunday morning entertainment and one Sunday Dave Short bought a dozen newspapers from the seller at the club door and gave one to each of the players:

"We sat in the front and when the stripper came on we all started reading our papers. She put up with it for five minutes then she started kicking the paper out of our hands."

At the end of the season the Byker Legion team went on a trip to Arenal in Spain, which was a major undertaking:

"Some of the lads had never been on a plane. Brian Spells was selling domino cards on the flight and when we got there we used to drink

in this bar called The Hole in the Wall, then we always went to this little bar beside the hotel for the last drink. Micky Coogan was always at the centre of things and the pub always had food on the counter. This night Coogie kept ordering drinks and every time the barman turned away Coogie took a huge bite out of this chicken. He ate half the chicken and the barman didn't know because he could only see the other half. One night we were going out as usual but Alan Renwick who was one of the older lads decided to stay in. When we got back he was well away and when the waiter came over to take the drinks order Renwick threw up all down the front of the bloke's white jacket. The waiter never flinched. He just picked the bits of carrot off his jacket and said, 'Will that be all sir?' "

While many of the team were on that holiday in Spain some had stayed behind and those who had stayed at home had the responsibility of playing in the last game of the season, which they had to win to clinch the league championship. Bob Shield, the club secretary, rang home to find out the result; when he managed to get through to the club phone, which was located in the doorman's cubby hole, and heard a voice say 'Benton club' he said 'This is Bob Shield.' 'Sorry mate,' came the reply, 'He's in Spain.'

It was at this time that Peter Feenan signed Billy for Newcastle Blue Star, where he formed a strike force with Ron Leman and Paul Dixon:

"Feenan was a great coach who taught me a lot about being a centre-forward and doing my damage in the opposing penalty area, but there was a lot of politics at Blue Star and I wasn't happy so I left for North Shields. It was a step up for me but the following season Blue Star won the FA Vase so maybe I should have stayed. I had no animosity, though; I was delighted that a team from the north-east had won it."

Billy (front, fourth from the left) and Micky Cogan (back, fifth from the left) at Fort Lauderdale, Florida USA

North Shields was a team in transition and Billy soon moved on to join Colin Richardson's Whickham. His big pals Micky Cogan and Jimmy Henderson were already there and he went across on training night to speak to Richardson:

"He called me over and took me for a chat — in the boiler room! I was overwhelmed by his ambition and I couldn't sign quickly enough. The amazing thing was that we won the first 11 games I played on the trot yet I never scored a goal, which was unknown for me; and I still finished up as top scorer that season.

"We won the league and got to the semi-final of the FA Vase, then Colin brought in Alan Scott from Consett; Micky Chapman was the driving-force in midfield and Dave Norton at full-back was 100% culture. We were playing

South Shields one Saturday and it was between us for the championship. Richardson was in his boiler room getting himself worked up, then he burst into the dressing room. 'Right,' he said, 'What do we know about South Shields?' and Dave North said, 'It's got a canny beach!'"

The following season brought a remarkable departure for Billy Cawthra when he was given the opportunity to play in the United States at Fort Lauderdale. Micky Cogan was already there and he had told them he was from Newcastle so they had assumed he meant Newcastle United. The structure at Fort Lauderdale was such that opportunities to play in the first team were virtually non-existent for Billy; there was a squad of 45 players which included his idol Gerd Muller as well as George Best, Gary Stanley, Keith Weller and the Cuban international Cubillas. Also in the side was the former Newcastle United player Ray 'Rocky' Hudson, who had played with Billy at Whickham. Billy played in the second string while training with the star names under the guidance of a Hungarian coach who had played with the legendary Puskas. Heady stuff indeed.

"It was an amazing experience in many ways. We were playing an Argentinian side under floodlights one night and every time I jumped to head the ball I felt this stabbing pain in my side. Their centre-half was sticking me with a hat pin but when I realised what was going on I sorted him out!"

So, from Fort Lauderdale back to the more mundane surroundings of Whickham and the 1980-81 season, which was to culminate in glory at Wembley in the FA Vase. Billy remembers the early regional rounds against teams from his own league as the hardest, and once they were safely negotiated things began to come together, and a settled side really began to buzz. The key player in the Vase run in Billy's estimation was Ian Diamond:

"Ian was superb but Colin Richardson wasn't too happy with his tackling so he brought him in for an extra training session. He made him lie down in front of every barrier around the pitch, then jump up and kick it with his studs. What a difference. Everything went through Ian, especially in the final."

In the round of the last 16 Whickham beat Thackley 2-0, with Billy Cawthra scoring both goals. He was then carried off and taken to hospital following an accidental collision with the Thackley goalkeeper. When he arrived at the hospital for treatment the doctor said:

"I'll be with you in a few minutes; I'm just listening to the end of the Whickham game on the radio!"

The team began to believe they could win the Vase when they played Devizes in the quarter-final. Adverse weather conditions caused the first game to be postponed and when the Devizes players turned up at the Glebe ground the following week to face Whickham on a sloping pitch in front of a baying crowd it was little surprise that Whickham won, especially with Micky Carroll having an inspired game on the wing:

"Micky was brilliant. At one point he sat on the ball, and the full-back lost control. He tried to kick him but Micky nutmegged him and left him on his backside. Great stuff."

The two-leg semi-final saw Whickham draw 1-1 at Windsor and Eton, with Billy again on target. The return leg, which attracted 4000 spectators to the Glebe, was a disappointing affair which went into extra time at 0-0, and it took a volley by Paul Allon from Billy's header to settle the tie. The Whickham players were paid a fiver each for reaching the final!

"The build-up to the final was great. We'd played in the final of the Shipowners Cup on the Monday night, and Keith Knox who was still at school had captained England schools against Scotland at Hampden Park on the Saturday. Hampden one week and Wembley the next. Amazing.

"Everything was fabulous. Micky Cogan flew in from America to see the game. I was nearly 30 then and I knew this was my one opportunity; everyone told me to savour every moment and I can remember everything. We were in the away dressing-room which had a huge team bath. Our mascot, a little lad who sadly died a couple of years later, led us out to a wall of black and white.

That winning goal at Wembley

My dad and brothers Rich and Jack were there, my mates from work and all of Whickham.

"We played Willinghall from Wolverhampton and they were a top side. After 15 minutes we were two down, then we pulled one back through Alan Scott from Ian Diamond's corner and we were back in it. I chased a through ball and caught the keeper on the temple. He went off and they finished the half with their centre-forward in goal.

"They changed the keeper in the second half and Ronnie Williamson scored a great equaliser in the top corner. I missed a very good chance to win it and the game went into extra time.

"Paul Allon came on for Keith Robertson and the ball was played down the line. Their centre-half, who had been outstanding, came across to cut it out but I pushed it past him and hit it towards the far corner of the goal, where Paul Allon was running in. The full-back got there first and tried to play the ball away. It came back towards me but I knew it was going in so I turned away with my arms up. If I had tapped it in I would have been credited with scoring the winner; as it was it went down as an own goal but it didn't matter — we'd won.

"We collected the cup and our medals then we went back to the dressing room and there was a bottle of beer waiting for us. We were in that big bath which was about ten feet deep and then

Celebrating victory in the FA Vase

there was a hell of a commotion and the dressing-room door opened and this kid who was a Whickham supporter in black and white came clashing in and jumped in the bath. He just wanted to be part of the celebrations but he didn't realise how deep it was. He disappeared and there was just this black and white hat floating on top of the water. I was last out of the dressing-room, still drinking it all in. I thanked the dressing-room stewards and they told me Colin Richardson had given them a tenner for their help; the first time they had ever had a tip in all their time at Wembley."

The team returned home in style. As the coach passed through Burnopfield they were greeted by one man and his dog, though to be fair the dog was wearing a black and white scarf. When they reached Whickham it was different; there were masses of people lining the high street and a huge gathering of supporters in the ground. Colin Richardson made a speech and Billy Cawthra's career had reached its pinnacle:

"It was a fairy tale and it's sad that they couldn't take it any further. I'm sorry to see them struggling now."

Billy went on to become player/manager at Dudley, where the Secretary Micky Richardson was a great help. They won the league and the Benevolent Bowl, then he moved to Washington and Bedlington Terriers before ending his league

Meeting the legendary Sir Matt Busby

career at the age of 39 with Forest Hall in the Northern Alliance. He still loves the game and is currently player/manager of Killingworth Over-40s at the Blue Flames club in Newcastle. He has great affection for the Over-40's, where he regards everyone as a star. Approaching his fiftieth birthday he still loves his involvement in the company of his great pals Mick Reynolds, Garry Brown, Dennis Mac and especially his brother and best friend Rich.

The last words on a highly successful career belong to a man who used them sparingly, Bill Cawthra senior, who followed Billy everywhere in his quiet and unobtrusive way. Never one to make false claims about his son's achievements he came home after one game in which Billy scored six goals for Northumberland and told his wife their son had had a 'canny game'.

On that memorable day at Wembley when Whickham won the Vase Mr. Cawthra travelled to London on the train as usual. The train was crowded but he managed to find a seat in a compartment which was occupied by a group of lads who said they were members of a band. It turned out that they were the world famous rock band AC/DC, whose lead singer, Brian Johnson, is a geordie. Brian later told Billy that at one point the conversation went like this:

"So you're in a band?"
"Aye"
"Any good?"
"Not bad."
"Have you played Coxlodge club?"
"No."
"You can't be any good if you haven't played Coxlodge club."
Great crack!

BILLY CRUDDAS

Holidays in September

A young Billy (front left) with Lambton & Hetton under-15's school team

Billy Cruddas never lacked family encouragement. As a diminutive five-feet-three-inches-tall schoolboy inside-forward, he was supported wherever he played by his father Tommy, with whom he shared a close bond, and his grandad Harry Talbot who used to say to him after every game:

"I'll tell you what it is. There was a bloke standing next to me today and he said: 'Who's that little blond lad? He's a good player.'"

It took Billy a long time to realise that this was just his grandad's way of encouraging him and boosting his confidence. Billy's early promise brought him to the attention of league club scouts, and at the age of 15 he went with Alan Foggon (later to win an Inter City Fairs Cup medal with

Newcastle United) to Bolton Wanderers, whose assistant manager was the legendary England centre-forward Nat Lofthouse. True to form, his dad and grandad went along and they were suitably impressed by their meeting with the 'lion of Vienna' and their visit to the Burnden Park boardroom:

> "This was 1966. My grandad had never been out of Herrington and when he saw the Bolton set-up he said: 'By, Billy, this is how the other half lives.'"

Those who know Billy Cruddas from his days as a non-league player and manager will be surprised to learn that he was a shy as well as a small 15-year-old who found life at Burnden Park overwhelming, and homesickness caused him to reject Bolton's offer of an apprenticeship. To the day he died Billy's dad carried in his wallet a letter from Bill Ridding, the Bolton manager, in which he expressed his regret that Billy felt unable to pursue his career at Burnden Park.

Back in junior football in the North East, his confidence in his playing ability undiminished, Billy turned out for Philadelphia juniors and as he grew from a small lad into a tall and gangly youth he switched, in his final year in junior football, to centre-forward and in the process broke the Houghton and District League goalscoring record with 77 goals. His goalscoring exploits brought him to the attention of Ferryhill Athletic, and at the age of 18 he joined a side which included Colin Richardson, who was to become a lifelong friend and, like Billy, an extremely successful manager.

He was in an out of the Ferryhill side as he came to terms with the demands of the Northern League, and after a two-year spell he joined Durham City at the age of 21:

> "I remember playing against Tony Monkhouse. He was a farmer and a real hard bastard. I was just a boy and it was the first time I ever got involved in a confrontation on the pitch. He said he would see me behind the clubhouse after the game; he probably said it ten times in a game, but I nearly shit myself. It made me realise what senior football in the Northern League was about."

Billy had two successful years at Durham City under the capable management of John Redhead, finishing as the club's leading goalscorer in both seasons, but controversy was to become something of a watchword in his career and it was after those two seasons at Ferens Park that he was banned from the Northern League for the first time.

Clubs were very reluctant to transfer players at that time and when he found out that the league's two leading teams, Blyth Spartans and North Shields, were after him but that Durham had not only kept him in the dark about their interest but had also refused to contemplate his transfer, he declined to play for them. In consequence he was banned from playing in the Northern League for the 1972-3 season and he joined Eppleton in the Wearside League, but after playing at Northern League level he found it difficult to motivate himself in what was then an inferior league. He remembers being on the substitutes' bench and being more interested in the horse-racing commentary on his transistor radio than he was in events on the pitch. So he returned to Durham to train and serve out his suspension.

The North Shields manager Jackie Marks renewed his interest in Billy, and Durham apparently agreed to his transfer, but one night when he was training at Shields' Appleby Park ground the news came through that they had changed their minds and the move fell through. Bitterly disappointed, he played a season in the local Saturday Morning league, but the standard was inadequate, so when Brandon United of the Northern Alliance offered to sign him he seized the opportunity:

"All the players like me who were barred from the Northern League were playing in the Alliance or the Wearside league, and the Alliance was a decent league with teams like Guisborough, Carlisle City and Seaham Red Star."

Billy played for Brandon for three seasons and whilst they were wilderness years to some degree, he regards his time there as the happiest of his career:

"John Heavysides was the manager; a real character. We weren't the best side but we had some good players. Peter Joyce was a great centre-half and we had Tommy Holden and Richie Madden. Willie White played outside-left because his right eye was missing and if he had played on the other wing he would have dunshed into the linesman."

Billy missed the start of the season due to suspension; he called it his usual September holiday, so frequently did he carry a suspension over from the previous season, but he quickly established himself, replacing Jock Rutherford at centre-forward.

In his second season at Brandon they were drawn away in the FA Cup Preliminary Round to a Tow Law Town side which included the future England star Chris Waddle:

"We beat them 4-0. I scored three headed goals though I wasn't great in the air. We went to South Bank and won 1-0 and in the third qualifying we beat Spennymoor 3-0, which was a massive result. We were drawn away to North Shields who were managed by the ex-Newcastle and Sheffield Utd player John Tudor. We were a village team playing one of the top amateur teams in the area. I would have killed to get through to the first round proper. It was a physical game and I clattered the keeper, a lad called Crisp. He bounced off the woodwork and had to be taken to hospital with a broken jaw, but the referee let it go and we scored and won the game 1-0."

That was the only occasion on which Billy's mother watched him play senior football; she was so dismayed by the physical nature of the game that she never watched another. There were three busloads of supporters from Brandon at the match and they were in high spirits, twice invading the pitch. In the clubhouse afterwards they were 'drinking for England' but when Billy went to order his pint the barman refused to serve him:

"'You're that big daft centre-forward; you're not getting served.' Ronnie Young played for Shields and even he said they would have to serve me."

Kenny Carr, the Brandon chairman, heard the commotion and when he discovered the cause he went back to the assembled Brandon supporters, ordered them to drink up, and led a mass exodus in support of Billy. John Tudor was quoted in the weekend press as saying that if that was non-league football he wanted nothing to do with it due to its excessively physical nature. Nevertheless, Brandon were through to the First Round proper, and they were drawn at home to Bradford. The game was played at Spennymoor United's Brewery Field ground and attracted a crowd of 4500. Brandon lost 3-0 but,

"It was a great day. We won the league three years running but that FA Cup tie was the highlight. Everyone was together at Brandon;

Billy (far right) on the attack for Brandon in the FA Cup

there were no divisions, it was just the happiest club. We applied for the Northern League and expected to be admitted but they turned us down. We had resigned from the league so we had to join the Tyneside Amateur League and all the good players left."

Billy took time out to go to Wembley at the end of that 1978 season to see Newcastle Blue Star win the FA Vase. He was staying in Barnet and on the night before the match he 'pulled' a local girl by telling her that he was playing at Wembley the next day. He arranged to meet her the following night and went to her house. Her father was on his way to a darts and dominoes presentation at his local social club, so they went along:

"Her father got on the mike and told everybody that one of the players from Wembley that afternoon was in the audience and he asked me to present some of the prizes! The blood drained

from my body and my knees buckled, but I had to carry it off."

After three years at Brandon the opportunity came to sign for Brian Newton at Bishop Auckland. John Heavysides, the Brandon manager, was upset but he was a good friend and didn't stand in Billy's way. Bishops came up with a good offer but Billy was going on holiday to Greece and he had lost his spending money in the betting shop the day before. He told Brian Newton he would sign if they gave him a £400 signing-on fee, and the next day he brought the money to the office where Billy was working:

"I came back from Greece looking like a bronzed god, but on the field I was a total embarrassment. I didn't enjoy it. I got off to a bad start and it wasn't my kind of club. We were playing Workington in the First Qualifying Round of the FA Cup and we stopped at this little place in the Lake District for lunch. I gulped my meal down and went straight to the betting shop. I had £10 on the winner of the one o'clock race at Newmarket at 25-1. I had £260 to pick up but the bookie wouldn't pay out until they had weighed in. The bus was leaving but I wasn't going without my money. Eventually I got it and jumped on the bus as it left the village. One of the committee said since I'd had such a good win I could pay the £30 I owed them for a new pair of boots. I peeled the money off the roll and paid him. Needless to say when we got to Workington I wasn't in the team and I was transferred to Chester le Street on the Monday. The next day I went to Brough Park dogs and lost all my winnings!"

After a disappointing first season at Chester le Street he came through in his second season to finish as leading goalscorer in a championship winning side before joining Colin Richardson at Newcastle Blue Star. Colin had brought his FA Vase-winning side to the Wheatsheaf Ground from Whickham, but their physical style didn't suit either the pitch or the chairman, Billy Dryden, who preferred good footballing sides to physical ones. By now Billy was 32 and he and Colin had been friends for many years, playing together in Sunday football. The side Richardson assembled at Blue Star was a formidable one containing the likes of John Swinburne, Tony Maggiore, Bill Lever, Ian Crumplin, Cuss Robson and Dave Callaghan. After a shaky start they carried all before them until they lost in the quarter-finals of the FA Vase to Shepshead Charterhouse:

"I cried that day. We were favourites even though they were a good side, but we lost 2-1 and I missed a sitter. I had been convinced that we were going to Wembley and I knew that at 32 I wouldn't get another chance."

Ironically, Blue Star were unbeaten for the rest of

Billy in the thick of it

that season, but Billy's chequered disciplinary record manifested itself in sendings off in the finals of the Shipowners Cup and the Northumberland Senior Cup.

The Northumberland FA came down heavily, taking into account his previous indiscretions, and banned him for a record 16 weeks:

"By November I was really depressed but Colin Richardson asked me to start training so that I could be ready for the Vase in January. I worked very, very hard and got into excellent condition, then they arranged a game against Coundon on my jinx ground at North Shields to help me get match fit. For the first 15 minutes this big ginger centre-half kicked me all over the pitch and the referee did nothing, but I knew I had to bite the bullet. Then I slid in for a tackle and missed and the ref. gave a free kick to Coundon. He called me over and sent me off. It was a terrible decision; I hadn't touched the player. The blood drained from my body, then the red mist came

Receiving his end-of-season Award from Brian 'Pop' Robson

offering him a coaching position shortly afterwards heralded the dawn of a new career. He had no coaching experience but adapted quickly and, because he stood up to the strong personality of Richardson, he gained the respect of the players. He worked as a coach at the Wheatsheaf for two years before moving into management with the Dunston Sunday Morning team. Billy had played for them since he was 19; the only Sunday team he played for, so it was an appropriate place to start his managerial career:

"Memories of Dunston are wonderful. As a player I was alongside the likes of Frankie Peareth, Freddy Shotton, Tommy Dixon, Tommy Robinson and Colin Richardson. We travelled to games in our own double-decker bus and our games against Byker Legion were legendary. There were huge crowds, sitting on crates of Brown Ale. I was the only outsider in the team when Colin took me. I never got paid, but once the engine seized on my car and they put a new engine in for nothing. The standard of football was remarkable."

down and I went for him. There was hell on. It was heartbreaking; I had been cheated and I knew it.

"At the disciplinary hearing four of the Coundon players said I hadn't touched the defender but they gave me an eight months ban and a £100 fine. It was headlines in the papers."

Billy's pal Ian Crumplin had accompanied him to the hearing at the Northumberland FA offices in central Newcastle and they decided to frighten the referee afterwards. Hiding in a shop doorway, they waited until the referee emerged then stepped out and walked towards him:

"He legged it back to the NFA offices and locked the door, so we went to the pub and got pissed."

That was the end of Billy Cruddas's playing career, but the generosity of Billy Dryden and Colin Richardson at Newcastle Blue Star in

Billy managed Dunston for a season and a half, during which time they won a cup and a league championship, reinforcing his belief in his managerial abilities. He moved to Vaux Breweries side as joint team manager with Tony Clark and again tasted success with victory in the prestigious Shipowners Cup before returning to his spiritual home at Durham City.

In his first spell as manager at Ferens Park, which lasted two years, he took them to promotion from the second division of the Northern League and to the quarter-finals of the FA Vase. One of his most significant signings was Whitley Bay goalkeeper Tony Harrison, who was to become his number two and ultimately his successor:

Dunston Social Club Sunday Team — close to Billy's heart

"I remember beating Tamworth in the Vase to reach the last eight. We only had nine men on the pitch when Peter Stronach scored the winner. I ran on the pitch at full time and one of my shoes stuck in the clarts 20 yards behind me. We could have won the quarter-final against Emley as well but I got the tactics wrong."

Billy's second season in charge saw Durham, who had no previous record of success, finish sixth in the first division of the Northern League, but at the end of the season he left for personal reasons and returned to Newcastle Blue Star as Colin Richardson's number two. After three or four games Colin received an excellent offer to manage North Shields, and Billy Dryden appointed Billy as his successor. Colin Richardson had naturally taken the key players with him to North Shields, but Billy nevertheless guided Blue Star to fifth and fourth positions in the league in successive seasons:

"We were training one night when I broke my finger: I caught it in Kevin Todd's track suit. I knew they weren't insured so I asked Billy Dryden what he was going to do about it. He doubled my money from then until the end of the season. Billy was a diamond, but the politics at the club were terrible and they began to get me down."

To his surprise, Durham City came back in for him, not knowing that he was growing weary of the politics at the Wheatsheaf Ground:

"I had all the bonny marbles. They must have wanted me badly because they didn't know I was unhappy at Blue Star. I got a wonderful deal and they even clapped me into the committee room. The hardest part was telling Billy Dryden after we had lost the League Cup Final at Gretna."

That second spell as manager of Durham City lasted six years, and from being second bottom of the second division of the Northern League, they won promotion in his first season, finished second in the top division, then won the championship. They were heady days, and there was the additional excitement of watching the new Durham City ground at New Ferens Park grow into an impressive reality.

The total commitment which had seen Billy Cruddas clash with authority throughout his career came through again at Chester le Street. Durham were sharing the Chester Moor ground while their new ground was under completion:

"The linesman got Billy Irwin sent off and there was an eruption near the corner flag. I ran around and got involved with the linesman and the referee said; "Mr Cruddas we would like you to leave the ground and the game won't restart until you do." I was sent out of the ground with 35 minutes to go so I climbed through the farmer's field and I was standing in the trees outside the ground watching. With 20 minutes to go I wanted to make a substitution but I couldn't

attract Tony Harrison's attention until the linesman said, He's up the tree.'

"I started waving my arms about to Tony and I fell out of the tree and into the beck! I was bloody drenched. Brian Honour was playing for me that day. He'd played a whole career in the football league and he reckoned he'd never seen anything like it."

After six very successful years at Durham City, the pressure of management began to take its toll on a man who gave it his all, and he began to fear for his health. All was not well at Durham and despite pleas from his senior players like Derek Bell and Brian Honour and his coach Tony Harrison, he told his players he intended to resign:

"It was very difficult. Everybody thought we had money but I had no budget. I'd brought them players and success that they couldn't have dreamed about but they didn't appreciate it or understand that sometimes a manager needs an arm around his shoulder and an encouraging word. There was one committee member in particular who made life difficult and I felt I couldn't continue. I've see two games since."

For someone as passionate about the game of football as Billy Cruddas to leave it in such a final way is a loss to the game, but he speaks without regret of his decision.

Billy Cruddas's passion these days is golf, and there is every possibility of him taking a golfing holiday in September. After all, he's used to taking his holidays at that time of year from his playing days.

IAN CRUMPLIN

Goals galore and midget gems

Joker in the pack

It's every schoolboy's dream to score the winning goal in a cup final at Wembley. Not only did Ian Crumplin fulfil his dream but he achieved it in the most dramatic of fashions, with a header in the last minute of the FA Vase Final of 1978 to bring victory to Newcastle Blue Star and to etch his name into non-league history.

It was apparent from an early age that 'Crumpy' was blessed with a unique talent for scoring goals. He first attracted the attention of the distinguished

North-East talent spotter Bill Emery on a rainswept Saturday morning when he was 12 years of age. A tiny lad, he caught the eye as he dashed past bigger defenders to score goals with apparently nonchalant ease. Emery was working as a scout for West Bromwich Albion at the time, and having decided that young Crumplin had something to offer he called at the house in Lemington in the west end of Newcastle where Ian lived with his father and two older brothers. The impish nature which was later to be used as a potent weapon to wind up opponents had manifested itself already, and when Bill Emery knocked at the door of the Crumplin household the youngster thought it was the father of some neighbourhood boy with whom he had been fighting on the school yard earlier in the day!

Crumplin went to West Bromwich Albion as a 13-year-old boy. He recalls being met at Newcastle Central Station to be taken to the Midlands for the first time:

> "They bought me steak and chips. I'd never had a meal like that in my life before and I can still remember it."

Mindful of his slight physique but encouraged by the fact that his mother was a relatively well-made woman, Bill Emery arranged for Ian to stay with the family of another aspiring youngster from the North East, Trevor Thompson, and with the benefit of regular meals and a balanced diet he began to develop the height and body strength his ambitions as a centre-forward required. In fact he matured as an adult to a height of 5 feet 10 inches. Sadly, however, things didn't work out at West Brom and Ian returned to the North East.

Apart from a season with Hartlepool United Crumplin played the bulk of his top-class football with Bill Dryden's Newcastle Blue Star side at the Wheatsheaf Ground in the shadow of Newcastle Airport. His goalscoring record for Blue Star was quite simply staggering. In ten seasons he scored a phenomenal 401 goals, (and if you let him, he'll describe them all for you).

The highlight was, of course, that winning goal against Barton Rovers in the final of the Vase, but the road to Wembley was, as might be expected with Crumpy involved, not without its bizarre moments.

Ian himself swears that it wasn't until the team reached the quarter-finals of the competition that he became aware that the final was played at Wembley. The FA Vase was a relatively fledgling competition in its fifth year and its profile wasn't especially high in publicity terms, so he could well be right.

In one of the earlier rounds of the competition Blue Star were drawn away to County Durham rivals Eppleton. Before the game player/manager Peter Feenan took the team to a local pub and ordered everyone a glass of sherry, presumably to stimulate an inner glow they could take on the pitch with them. Crumpy, though, is an individual. He didn't drink the sherry because he didn't like it, but scored the only goal in a 1-0 victory.

The fifth round saw the team drawn at home to a side from the Sheffield area called Frenchville, but Crumpy had a problem. The only pair of football boots he possessed were split, so with his team-mate Paul Dixon in tow he went into a cobbler's shop on Newcastle's Gosforth High Street and announced:

> "I'm playing for Blue Star in the FA Vase this afternoon. Can you do anything with these?"

Whilst the other customers in the shop wished

Newcastle Blue Star's FA Vase winning squad

him luck in the game the boots were duly repaired, free of charge, and Frenchville were disposed of as Blue Star took another step towards Wembley.

There was another extraordinary incident on the away leg of the semi-final when the advance party who had been sent to plan the route and were therefore the only Blue Star people who knew the way to the ground, unaccountably travelled on the supporters' bus. That bus became separated from the team coach, whose driver had no local knowledge and was driving away from the ground. Chairman Billy Dryden, realising that time was running out, flagged down a car driver who turned out to be a local. Billy pressed £20 into the man's hand and demanded that he accompany them to the ground: as a consequence

they arrived 25 minutes before kick-off having changed on the coach.

One of Crumpy's most endearing characteristics was that he invariably brought a large supply of sweets for general consumption on long away trips. Apart from one occasion when he had been asked to provide some mints and turned up with half a pound of mince, he never failed to produce the goods. On semi-final day he unveiled a seven-pound box of 'Midget Gems'.

> "By the end of the journey me jaws were aching and I finished up hoying them at everybody on the bus."

So to Wembley and that goal. Barton scored first; Barry Dunn, later to play for Sunderland,

Champagne celebrations at Wembley

equalised and it was 1-1 at half time. A missed penalty prevented Blue Star from going ahead. Crumpy takes up the story:

"I didn't realise how little time there was left. I thought there was about 20 minutes to play but it was the last minute. I don't think Barton touched the ball. Bobby Halbert threw the ball to Feenan. Peter passed to Peter Davidson and he raced away down the right wing and crossed. Paul Dixon went to the near post and I came running in and headed it into the net from about 12 yards. I got a lot of power on the header and I knew it was going in. I didn't realise the

Blue Star FC — Guests of the Lord Mayor of Newcastle at the Mansion House

significance of it straight away but as soon as the final whistle went I was in cuckoo land. There were a lot of young lads in the team and I don't think we realised what we had done. We didn't really take in the occasion. Now, we're remembered forever."

There was one ironic footnote, literally, and it concerned that pair of boots which had been repaired before the fifth round game:

"They finally clapped out at half-time in the final so I changed my boots at half-time and scored the winner. With a header!"

So it's as an extraordinary goalscorer and a man

who fulfilled every schoolboy's dream that Ian Crumplin is remembered, but he also has a place in non-league folklore as a character, a wind-up merchant, a player with an impish sense of fun and a talent for talking himself into trouble.

Take for instance his love/hate relationship with manager Colin Richardson, himself one of the game's most colourful and successful non-league managers. After scoring a goal against Chester le Street Crumpy started turning somersaults. The angrier Colin Richardson's expression became in the dug-out the more Ian persisted, and he somersaulted all the way back to the centre spot! On another occasion Blue Star were playing an away game against Roker, who were bottom of the league, and Crumplin scored six goals in a 9-0 victory. The following Monday night they were playing South Shields and before the kick-off Crumpy fell into conversation with the Shields centre-half Paul Hedley in the toilets.

"Why did you have to score six on Saturday? I've got to man-mark you tonight."

"Aye, but did you know that at half-time after I'd scored five in the first half I got a bollocking off Richardson for not tracking back after a full-back who'd gone on a forward run? Stupid bastard. He can chase himself if he thinks I'm going to chase back when I've scored five goals."

During the team talk before kick-off Richardson turned to Crumplin and said:

"And if the full back goes on a run you WILL chase back. I go to the toilet too you know."

The manager had been sitting in a toilet cubicle and heard every word of Crumpy's tirade!

It's typical of Crumplin that he was never sent off for swearing at a match official but he was sent off three times for swearing at Colin Richardson in the dug-out. In fact, he had a good rapport with referees and respected them for the most part. He didn't always show the same restraint where his fellow players were concerned.

 He routinely cut off shirt buttons and ends of ties, and even Trevor Brooking was one of his victims. Brooking played a game as a guest for Blue Star, and Ian, believing that Brooking would turn up wearing either grey or navy blue socks, took a pair of each colour to the game having first cut off the toes. He substituted the appropriate colour for Brooking's own so that when Trevor came to get changed after the game he found himself with a pair of socks with no toes in them. It didn't take him long to identify the culprit, assisted as he was by the knowledge that Crumpy had hung two hammers over the dressing-room door and gone around before the game blowing bubbles from a child's bubble-pipe to make the former West Ham player feel at home!

Those ten years at Newcastle Blue Star were tremendously fulfilling for Ian Crumplin, followed by successful years at Whitley Bay football club and North Shields. He also experienced success and happy times prior to Blue Star when he played for two years for the former Whitley Bay stalwarts Billy Wright and Kenny Sloan at Ashington. Once again the Crumplin sense of humour was very much to the fore, not least in the incident of Billy Wright's tracksuit.

"Billy Wright was 6'2" and built like a brick shithouse. His wife always packed his training kit and one night when we were training it was pissing down with rain so I pinched his tracksuit and hid it. When he couldn't find it he went wild and said he would give his wife a right mouthful when he got home. After training I put his

Receiving his Player-of-the-Month Award at Hillheads, Whitley Bay, helped by his daughter, Elaine

tracksuit back in his bag. When he got home he started to bollock his wife who swore that she had put the tracksuit in his bag. He opened it up and found it. 'I'll kill that bastard Crumplin', he said. I couldn't blame him really."

Ironically, Ian himself didn't possess a tracksuit at the time and he recalls with great affection the fact that the training staff at Ashington bought him one out of their own pockets:

"They were great at Ashington. I remember when Steve Locker made his first-team debut

he bandaged his ankles because he saw another player doing it and thought that was what first-team players did. He tied them so tight he couldn't kick a ball straight in the first half. He took them off at half-time and had a much better second half. I wouldn't have left Ashington if they hadn't sacked Billy Wright, but then I probably wouldn't have gone to Wembley."

An accident with a bandsaw at work resulted in Ian losing two fingers, and on particularly cold days he wore protective woollen gloves. He used to cut the two fingers out of the gloves and sew them up so that they fitted, but he didn't tell that to Alan Gates who was substitute on one occasion and asked to borrow Crumpy's gloves. He couldn't understand how they wouldn't fit his hand! Incidentally, those missing fingers caused the Ashington supporters to produce a variation on the 'Crumpy' nickname: they called him 'Stumpy'!

So that's Ian Crumplin. A man who played the game with a smile on his face but who didn't like to lose and never joked when things were not going well on the pitch. A man who resented the suggestion that he was not a good trainer:

> "I only missed one training session in 20 years. I was fit and I enjoyed training, even at Ashington where I had to wait in the bar after training while Billy Wright and Kenny Sloan drank several pints of beer. While I was waiting I would have six Mars Bars, six packets of crisps and six cokes, then they would give me a lift to Newcastle where I got the last bus home at 11 o'clock."

The wheel has come full circle for Crumpy; he now earns his living as a bus driver!

In his long and distinguished career Ian suffered only two significant injuries, both to knee ligaments. He did cause his wife Connie to worry on one occasion when he was watching, of all things, 'Your Life in Their Hands' on television. She came into the room and found him grey and sweating profusely. She couldn't find any pulse and he didn't respond when she started to slap his face. Panic-stricken she ran screaming to her neighbours and called an ambulance. When she came back he was walking round the room. He spent four days in hospital having tests which revealed nothing beyond the fact that he had the very slow heartbeat of a top-class athlete. He has had no problems in the eight years since that incident and still lives life with a smile on his face but with a serious demeanour when the situation requires it.

In 1993 Ian played for Ponteland United in the Northern Alliance. In their FA Vase run that year he scored 11 goals in five rounds of the competition including the preliminaries, before they lost 1-0 at Burscough. One of the home crowd said to him after that game, "You've got a tidy little side there; all you need is a goalscorer!"

However, Ian had the last laugh and enjoyed another immensely proud moment at the end of that season. At the Sportswriters Dinner at the Three Tuns Hotel in Durham, a lavish affair attended by such luminaries as Kevin Keegan and Sir John Hall, he received the Goalscoring Achievements Award for his scoring prowess, including the little matter of 59 he scored for Ponteland that season. He became only the second non-league player to be so honoured, the first having been Bishop Auckland legend Bob Hardisty.

So next time you take a bus on Tyneside, pay the driver some respect as well as your fare. You could be talking to a legend: a man who scored the winner in the last minute of a cup final at Wembley.

PETER FEENAN

Glasses of sherry and coaching skills

A young Peter Feenan (front, second from left) with St. Mary's Boys' Club

Peter Feenan was slight of build as a youngster and despite a high level of ability he found it difficult to cope with the hurly-burly of school football, and it wasn't until he left school and joined St. Mary's Boys Club at the age of 16 that he began to develop as a fully rounded player. It was a major step for a Gateshead lad who had

never been to Newcastle to join a team in the Scotswood area of the city, but he had committed himself to a good club which was run by Jimmy Fraser and Norman Heaney, and which included among its players Norman Lees and Brian Chambers, who went on to play for Darlington and Sunderland respectively. A member of the

Northumberland County side was Albert Aiston, whose son Sam was also to become a Sunderland player; Albert and Peter were later to join Blyth Spartans together, but not before a successful period at St. Mary's locking horns with their principal rivals from Montagu and North Fenham and West End boys' clubs.

It was after a cup final at Hunter's Moor, the old Newcastle United training ground, that Peter was approached by the top man at Blyth Spartans, Jimmy Turney, and invited to sign:

"It was a big game and we had a good side. Alan Saunders who went on to be a top referee played in goal. Turney came to watch and he signed Albert and me after the game. It was a magical move for me because my dad had played with Jimmy Turney at Blyth. Actually I played four games with my dad for The Bugle on Sundays but I was too young to be allowed in the bar after the game. I remember shouting 'Dad, dad' when I wanted the ball and him telling me I could call him Peter on Sundays."

Peter trained with Blyth Spartans that close season, and training nights were far from straightforward for a lad who lived in Gateshead and worked on the town's Team Valley trading estate. After work he caught a bus to Newcastle's Haymarket bus station to meet the 6:30 for Blyth, and he repeated this process twice a week for three months before he knew people well enough to ask for a lift. His Spartans debut came as a result of an injury to Tommy Orrick:

"Tommy was a prolific goalscorer but he was like Lord Snooty — he always wanted the ball laid on. His injury meant that I made my debut in the FA Cup against Bishop Auckland, who were managed by Lawrie McMenemy. Blyth were a professional team operating in the North Eastern League and if I was in the team I would get a telegram on a Saturday morning, which was quite something. I then had to get to St. Dominic's Church in Newcastle to meet the team bus. I thought it was big time."

Peter was an established player in the Blyth team in his second season and he stayed there until he was 23, playing in a side which didn't win any significant trophies but which was always a good and well-supported team with players of the calibre of Eddie Alder, Peter Flaherty, Geordie Little and Mike Hind in the line-up. However, Peter testifies that it was always Jimmy Turney's team irrespective of who was the manager, and the day came when Peter fell out with Turney and Jackie Marks and left the club:

"I was out of the team in spite of the fact that I was playing well and getting man-of-the-match awards from opposing players. I received a phone call from Charlie Thomas at Shildon so I went there. Charlie was a superb bloke; he fined you for swearing but he knew a player and he also recognised which players would complement each other. He was a man of dignity, which I admired."

Peter spent a season and a half at Shildon and then moved to Spennymoor to play for Billy Bell, but Shildon objected and had him banned from playing in the Northern League:

"It was a pity because Spennymoor were a very good side. Billy Bell's physical training was good and he had a strict and rigid playing method. He was particularly good at improving average players."

The ban which prevented Peter from playing in the Northern League caused him to leave Spennymoor and move to Gateshead, where he played under Jimmy Rayner and then the former Newcastle United striker Ron McGarry in a side

Early days at Blyth Spartans (Peter back row third from left)

which included outstanding players like Harry Godbold and Gerry Coyne. Ron McGarry's approach to management was a highly individual and cavalier one; it was not unknown for him to stop the team bus at a betting shop on the way to away fixtures, and despite playing in the prestigious Northern Premier League the club's financial position was a precarious one:

"On away days the coach picked us up at the

Springfield Hotel and we always stopped at the same hotel for lunch. The fifth week the manager wouldn't let us in because his bill hadn't been paid, and another time we were waiting at the Springfield for the coach to take us to Boston but it didn't turn up because the company was owed money. It was like that all season."

Peter, by now approaching 25 years of age, moved on after a season to play for Tow Law, who were managed by another distinguished former professional in the shape of the ex-Spurs and Arsenal star Laurie Brown. He had been an outstanding player but in Peter's judgement, despite producing a good team he never came to terms with the requirements of the non-league game. He was also a man of few words:

"He only ever spoke to me once. We were playing on this heavy pitch at Tow Law and after the game he said to me; 'I remember playing Chelsea on a heavy pitch and Jimmy Greaves

Peter (front row, left) as a young player/manager at Tow Law

came off like you — clean as a whistle.' That's all he ever said except for a time at Evenwood. Their centre-half was Colin Hallimond who was a fabulous player and a gentle giant. Brown told us nothing would upset him. Well, I was five yards out and I launched myself and put the ball and the keeper in the back of the net; Hallimond knocked me out, and Brown just said: 'I am surprised.' He didn't come back the next season."

Laurie Brown's departure provided Peter with his first opportunity in management. His assiduous interest in the coaching side of the game, which has been the motivating force behind his years of success in non-league management, had already manifested itself, and he possessed his FA preliminary coaching badge. He assembled a good side which included Tony Brunton:

"The craziest goalkeeper ever, but he played for England"

as well as Billy Skelly, Barry 'Badger' Robinson from Ashington, Barry Dunn and Robbie Hall from Silksworth, and a fabulous player from Gateshead called Derek Mercer:

"They were great lads, but lunatics. Anyway, we won the Northern League cup, beating Ashington in the final. It was Tow Law's first trophy for years."

Peter Feenan was in his element. He combined playing with coaching and found that he could influence and help players that way much more effectively than he could from the touch-line. Situations arose in games to which he could respond in a real way; there was none of the artificiality of the training ground. Unfortunately, at the end of his second season in charge at Tow Law a situation arose to which he took exception. The committee wanted to bring in someone to help

Peter run the team; he regarded this as interference which he couldn't tolerate, so he felt compelled to move on. Joining another Tow Law player, Terry Hunt, he played Sunday football for the Newcastle Black Bull pub side which was run by Billy Dryden and which was the embryo of Newcastle Blue Star:

"Billy Dryden used to watch Tow Law and he took me to Newcastle Blue Star, who had just joined the Wearside League, as player/manager. I brought in quality players to supplement what was an expanding club. Another plus was the fact that they had a very good playing pitch and that suited me because I always encouraged quality football. Billy Dryden was a wonderful man whose impact on non-league football in the North East was tremendous. Mind you, he had an obsession with centre-forwards. He would have had eleven in the team if he could."

Newcastle Blue Star was a talented team which included Joe Armstrong, whose brother David was a stalwart at Middlesbrough, Alan Chapman, Billy Cawthra and Ronnie Leman, but whilst that first Feenan-managed team proved its quality by winning the Northumberland Senior Cup, Peter believed that too many of the players were too parochial in their attitude and were unable to produce their best form when they travelled to unfamiliar surroundings, so it was something of a blessing that the team broke up at the end of that first season, presenting him with an opportunity to build his own team geared for success. He did so to devastating effect, producing a side which won the FA Vase at the first time of asking; a monumental achievement for a young and relatively inexperienced player/manager in his twenties.

Peter brought in Alan York as his assistant, which proved to be a masterstroke:

'We're on our way to Wembley' — celebrating the semi-final win

"He was a quiet lad but we hit it off superbly. He was the ideal buffer for me and because he had played pro he saw things I couldn't see or didn't want to see, particularly defensively."

Quality players were also recruited; Eric Ross, an Irishman who had been with Newcastle United, a young strike force comprising Ian Crumplin and Paul Dixon, winger Barry Dunn who went on to success at Sunderland. Jimmy Thompson came in and right-winger Peter Davidson was beginning to blossom, while Steve Dixon, who had been released by Bolton Wanderers, became another vital piece of the jigsaw. It was a young side but it quickly became apparent that it was also an outstanding footballing side which was playing below its level in the Wearside League. Peter, like most managers, had begun to develop his own small idiosyncrasies which became part of the Blue Star match routine:

"Before the first Vase game against Eppleton I gave then all a glass of sherry and that became an established routine."

Adaptability has always been a vital ingredient of Peter Feenan's approach to coaching and tactics, and this was never better illustrated than in the FA Vase replay against Brigg Town. Alan York had done his usual spying job on the opposition and produced a meticulous report which highlighted the talent of the Brigg right-back, who was sensational in the away tie but had confirmed his inability to head the ball in defensive situations, which Alan York had noted. Consequently, Peter switched striker Paul Dixon, who was strong in the air, to outside-left and instructed his midfield players to feed him with crossfield passes. The ploy worked like a charm and as a direct result of this tactical awareness Brigg Town, who were favourites to win the Vase, were 4-0 down at half time and lost the tie 8-0:

"I expected to win every game so it wasn't as big a surprise to me as it was to everyone else. I knew the tactics were right and I knew I had a very good team. I also knew that when the chips were down I had somebody like Frankie Storey in midfield who couldn't run but was a great player. By the time we reached the semi-finals the committee was worried that we would not make it to Wembley, but I didn't believe that any team could beat us over two legs."

The team had arrived at their hotel at ten o'clock on the evening prior to their first leg semi-final match and Peter told his players they could go out for a drink to help them relax, coupled with a warning that any player who failed to return by midnight would not be considered for selection the next day. His decision to let the players have a drink was met with considerable disapproval by chairman Billy Dryden, whose blood pressure wasn't helped by two of the players, Barry Dunn and Jimmy Thompson, hiding around the corner and coming in as the clock was striking midnight:

"I had to make some tough decisions; I left out Paul Dixon and Barry Dunn in that away leg but the decision was justified when we beat them 3-1. I had a poor game down there myself: Alan York had warned me that their left-winger was good. I wasn't a tough player but Steve Dixon was, so I told him I would show the player the line and he should be ready to nail him. Steve launched himself, missed the player and knocked over eight spectators. The winger roasted me!"

It would be reasonable to assume that having taken his side to the final of the 1978 FA Vase Peter would relish every moment of the gradual build-up between the semi-final and the big day, but the reverse was the case. There was a lot of tension among players who wondered if they would be in the side, and Peter himself was playing — which increased the pressure on the manager:

"It was a fraught time and I was glad when we finally got to Wembley for the match. I believe I picked myself on merit and my influence on Peter Davidson in the game was a crucial factor in our win. Ian Diamond was left out but thankfully he became a Vase winner later with Whickham. Alan York led the team out in recognition of his contribution, and we beat Barton Rovers 2-1."

Peter Feenan is a phlegmatic character and he

didn't spend time wallowing in the glory of FA Vase success. It was a job well done and he took satisfaction from that, but there was another season to prepare for and Peter was keen to develop his expertise and his love of coaching, so he spent part of the close season taking his full FA coaching badge at Houghall College in Durham City. The residential course lasted two weeks and it was extremely intensive. John Tudor and Willie McFaul from Newcastle United were fellow course members, and Peter's group was under the supervision of Howard Wilkinson:

"They needed to be convinced that you were of good and strong character so they put you under pressure. You were given an assignment relating to some aspect of coaching and you had to prepare and deliver a session the next day. Wilkinson would walk up and down the touchline with his clipboard and you had to respond to his 'stop, stand still' command. He slaughtered one bloke who broke down in tears — that was him out, but it was the best fortnight I ever had in my life."

Peter spent five years at Blue Star and he found consistent satisfaction in the club's ability to attract good players. He describes working with good players as his greatest pleasure, and there is no doubt that coaching and helping players to improve is his greatest love and his greatest talent. In the end, though, he fell out with Billy Dryden and after five happy years he moved on. Still only 35, he went to Durham City who were struggling but who, with patience, could have made more progress. The patience wasn't there so Peter moved to Brandon with Ray Gowans as his assistant:

"Bobby Kerr from Sunderland was in the side. He came for 15 quid a game and he was a marvellous character. Warren Teasdale and Dean

Happy days at Blyth Spartans (Peter standing on the right)

Gibb were there and so was Willie Moat, who was so keen he was playing four weeks after having his appendix out. He nearly collapsed in his comeback game; I gave him a plaster to stick over the wound! I wouldn't have left Brandon for anywhere except Blyth Spartans, so when Jackie Marks came and offered me the Blyth job and the chance to work with top-class players I went. Alan York rejoined me and he was a great ally. The first night's training I took three bags of balls out — Marksie couldn't believe it but I loved it."

Players invariably respond to Peter's methods and his team at Blyth was no exception. Dave Clarke, the former Newcastle United goalkeeper, was a case in point. He was a top-class keeper but because of his relative lack of height he was reluctant to come out for crosses. Peter did a session with him on crosses which Clarke acknowledged was better than anything he had experienced at Newcastle.

Peter believes that nothing he has done in football compares with his time at Blyth, a club where the manager is always under immense pressure but one which Peter was convinced was top-class and one where he achieved success. Change is part of football and when Alan York moved on Peter brought in another tested number two in Derek Middleton and the success continued:

"Things began to go wrong in the fifth season. It really started when we were playing at Seaham and the chairman came to the dug-out and told me I was making a so and so of him by not playing his son. The lad was a good player but he wasn't worth his place on a regular basis. By then end of the season I had taken the team to promotion and the final of the Senior Cup, and this was after being told at the start of the season that the aim was consolidation because money was short. The position became untenable."

After the Blyth experience Peter became something of an itinerant manager, spending a season and a half at Ashington with Keith 'Bruno' Brown as his assistant. He worked with good players at Portland Park despite the fact that it was a struggling club. Ronnie Rutledge, the Chairman, Micky Gibson, Artie Lumsden, Robbie Dunbar, Micky Richmond and Davie Matthews were all there; players with ability who were improved by Peter Feenan. However, it wasn't Blyth and he found it difficult to stay focused. After Ashington there was a brief spell at Ryhope, the highlight of which was the opportunity to work with Colin Cowan, whom Peter rates as the best striker he ever coached.

His next really fulfilling post, though, was with Gretna:

"It was brilliant. I liked the Cumbrians and I had a good relationship with Willie Armstrong and Geoff Fell who ran the club. I took Paul Ross, Lawrence Hardwick and Colin Cowan across and they did a good job for me. They were a relegation-threatened side when I went and in the two-and-a-half years I was there I turned them into a respectable team."

From Gretna he went to help out at South Shields and he had success there during his short stay, but when the club threatened to fine him four weeks wages for going on a week's holiday he decided that discretion was the better part of valour and, in a direct swap with Bobby Graham, became manager of Morpeth Town:

"I've had a marvellous time at Morpeth. When I arrived at the club I inherited three exceptional young players. Kevin Henderson was a willing horse with a big heart and I worked on getting him to play facing the goal because with his back to goal his touch would let him down. It worked like a charm and we were murdering teams. He

Peter (left) with his successful Sunday team — Framwellgate Moor

went to Burnley when Chris Waddle and Glenn Roeder were there. Another was John Cullen, and Mick Tait signed him for Hartlepool. He was subsequently sold to Sheffield United for £250,000. Then there was Jon Atkinson who was desperate to be a professional. He went to Darlington on transfer deadline day but he didn't make it. If he had been a bit more patient he could have done better because he had a lot of talent."

So Peter Feenan has done well for Morpeth Town and brought a smile to the face of the Chairman, Ken Beattie, as well as creating opportunities for young players to make their way in the professional game. Over the years he has given North-East non-league football a great deal, and he has indulged his passion for coaching good players. His major pleasure and ambition these days is to develop young talent — which he does with wisdom and compassion. If young players want to improve and learn their craft they should make a beeline for Peter Feenan. He has left Morpeth to take up what he says will be his final challenge as coach at Shildon. At the end of his spell there he intends to move to Spain and enjoy a well-earned rest.

DEAN GIBB

A quiet prayer and the odd red card.

Dean Gibb — Young Gladiator!

The football world first became aware of the name of Dean Gibb when he broke into the Newcastle Boys under-13 side as a defender, and the behaviour which has made him a character throughout his career soon manifested itself:

"We went on a weekend tour to Scotland to play Edinburgh Boys and Musselburgh Boys. Ian Bogie and Paul Stephenson, who both made it into Newcastle United's first team, were in the squad and we stayed in this unfinished hostel outside Edinburgh. It was freezing and each bunk had six blankets. The water in the showers was so cold I didn't get washed all weekend. When I got home my clothes were stinking."

Dean continued to catch the eye in local representative matches and he was invited by George Ormond to play for Montagu and North Fenham Boys Club. Scouts from professional clubs always watched Montagu's matches against their principal rivals Wallsend Boys Club and Cramlington Juniors, and Dean was invited for trials by several clubs before signing schoolboy forms with Ipswich Town shortly before his fourteenth birthday. Bobby Robson left the manager's job shortly afterwards to take up the England post, and the former Newcastle United defender Bobby Ferguson took over:

"There were some good lads from the North-East there; David Robson, Keith Gorman, Anthony Hulme, Micky Stockwell and Gary West, but I was released after two seasons. I actually stopped playing for a while but I wouldn't let my disappointment beat me and I started playing again for Montagu and for Lemington Social Club on a Sunday morning with Warren Teasdale and Peter Feenan."

Having left school and started working on a YTS scheme, young Dean was invited by Peter Feenan to play for Brandon United, initially in the Midweek Floodlit League, his debut coming against Hartlepool in a team which included ex-Sunderland skipper Bobby Kerr and Dean's pal Warren Teasdale in midfield. His junior football days were virtually over now, and despite the opportunity to follow Peter Feenan to Blyth Spartans he elected to stay at Brandon to play under their new manager Ray Gowans, who was to find a new role for Dean and give his career a considerable boost:

"He started playing me left-back but I wasn't playing particularly well and Ray decided to play me up-front with Brian Jennings, who scored millions of goals. I was a bit taken aback but we tried it in the Floodlit League against Billingham Town. Willie Moat and Neil Howie were on the wings so the service was great. I scored one and made three and we beat them 5-1. The partnership with Brian Jennings gelled from day one."

Dean Gibb could never be described as a shrinking violet and his antics were as likely to irritate his team-mates as the opposition. Take for example the occasion when the team was returning on the coach from a match at Bridlington:

"I was working myself as usual in the back of the bus so Willie Moat, Steppy Dixon, Keith 'Bruno' Brown and Jock Thompson grabbed hold of me. They took my tie and wrapped it round my neck and my privates then they put sellotape round it and pulled it off. As you can imagine I was in agony."

Dean was seventeen-and-a-half now and playing with the huge self-confidence which is his hallmark. Liverpool and Coventry City both looked at him but advised a further year at Brandon gaining experience. Then, in a game against Hartlepool Reserves in which he was marked by David Linighan (later of Arsenal), he scored two outstanding goals. An invitation for trials at Hartlepool followed and, unwilling to wait another season for Liverpool or Coventry, he signed for Hartlepool for a fee of £750:

"Brandon were great about it. I met John Smart the Hartlepool chairman and Billy Horner the manager at the Dixielanders in Leam Lane and they offered me decent terms and a £500 signing-on fee. I talked it over with my dad, put my notice in at work and signed as a professional with Hartlepool on Tuesday 14th June 1986. I'm still waiting for the £500!"

In two seasons with Hartlepool Dean scored 15 goals, some from midfield, and he remembers as the highlight a 1-1 draw with Middlesbrough of the First Division in the Littlewoods Cup. Middlesbrough's team included Bernie Slaven, Tony Mowbray and Brian Laws, and Hartlepool were unlucky to go down 2-1 in the replay:

"Our longest journey was to Torquay and Exeter and we played them over the same weekend in October. Ten of us went collecting conkers in the hotel grounds but Ray Hogan had stayed in his room so we sneaked up to his window and pelted him with conkers. He was reading a porn magazine and we'd caught him red-handed."

Flying high for Bedlington Terriers

Hartlepool weren't playing Dean regularly, but they wouldn't let him go out on loan, so he was doubly aggrieved when they released him:

"I wasn't very happy. I threw my boots on the manager's table and walked out, then I thought 'Hang on, those boots cost £100,' so I went back for them, then I signed for Brandon again for £50 a week."

Now 21, Dean's confidence was at a low ebb, so

he reverted to right-back, a position he knew, and began to rebuild his career. Playing against Blyth Spartans his old brashness was starting to return and he went on a run past two players to lay on a goal. The consequence of his exuberance in celebrating the goal was a confrontation with Jimmy Harmison which ended with two of Dean's front teeth lying on the pitch in front of him.

Billy Horner, his old gaffer at Hartlepool, was now

managing Seaham Red Star on a decent budget and Dean signed for him:

"He was a nice lad. It was a good team and a good time. Mick Smith who went to Wimbledon and did very well was there and so were Willy Ferry and Ged Parkinson. We went to play in a pre-season tournament in Holland and late one night we all sitting totally naked in this bar absolutely drunk. The team we were playing in the tournament final the next day had set us up but it didn't matter because I play better when I'm drunk anyway and we beat them easily."

Dean had two on-and-off seasons at Seaham — literally. He had developed a reputation for getting into trouble on the field, partly because of the arrogance which is part of his make-up as a player, and red cards have littered his career fairly liberally.

There followed what was the worst period in Dean's chequered career: a short, unhappy spell at Spennymoor, and a return to Seaham where he broke his leg and missed virtually a whole season. There was another short spell at Spennymoor with Mattie Pearson and David 'Dick' Barton before the clouds lifted when he joined Durham City to play for Billy Cruddas and form a highly successful partnership up front with Micky Taylor:

"Micky and I were getting treatment one night and we sneaked two bottles of bubble-bath into the team bath at Ferens Park. We shook it up for ages and when the players came in from training the dressing room was full of foam and there was Micky sitting in the middle of it like Barbara Cartland. Another time Micky and I sneaked off the training pitch and ran back on bollock-naked. Billy laughed so much his teeth fell in the mud."

On another occasion Billy Cruddas stormed into the dressing room to issue a half-time tirade but he only got as far as "You f..." when his teeth flew across the dressing room. Thereafter, when he wanted to shout at his players he put his fingers on his front teeth.

After a game against Workington in the FA Vase Dean felt that Billy was unjustified in criticising his performance in front of the other players and he decided to move on. Opportunely, he had started to work for a new company and he was at the Northumberland Plate meeting at Newcastle Racecourse enjoying their hospitality:

"I bumped into Steve Locker and he introduced me to Dave and Keith Perry in the Champagne Bar. They had revived the fortunes of Bedlington Terriers and Keith asked me to sign for them. We agreed terms straight away.

"I really felt comfortable with the Perry brothers and we shook hands on the deal. They gave me a bottle of champagne and I was a Bedlington player. I wanted to play for them and they wanted me. Durham City set up a transfer deal whereby when Bedlington bought their old floodlights Micky Taylor and I were part of the package."

As usual, Dean was suspended for the first game of the new season but he soon took his place in a team which already included John Sokaluk, Andy Gowans, Warren Teasdale and Tommy Ditchburn. In his debut game at Welfare Park they defeated Billingham Synthonia 5-1, and Dean's combative and skilful contribution made him an instant crowd favourite. That first season the Terriers finished fourth in the Northern League and Dean was putting down roots. John Milner was signed as a goalscoring midfield player and Dean was partnered up-front variously by Richie Bond, Mark Cameron and

Don Peattie. However, the stars decreed that John Milner and Dean Gibb should play together as a strike force and their hugely successful pairing began the following season.

From the start they developed an almost telepathic understanding and it was in that same season that Bedlington's love affair with the FA Vase began when they reached the quarter-finals, where they

Terriers Dynamic Duo — John Milner (left) and Dean

lost to North Ferriby despite hitting the woodwork three times. Ferriby went on to lose to Whitby Town in the final.

Three magical seasons followed. Gibb and Milner scored over 200 goals between them, the Northern League championship was won three times and there was an unforgettable trip to Wembley as well as a heart-gladdening run in the FA Cup. The 1998-99 season was the highlight not only of Dean Gibb's career but the greatest season by far in the history of Bedlington Terriers. In five years Keith and David Perry, as manager and chairman, took the club from the brink of extinction to the paths of glory, and that season will live forever in the memory.

The pre-season build-up was good and when they began the real action with a 3-1 win over Dunston in the final of the Cleator Cup the ball began to roll. The Gibb-Milner partnership came together again with John moving up from midfield against Pickering Town in the preliminary round of the FA Cup; the outcome was an 8-1 victory with Milner scoring four and Dean completing a hat-trick. Next came Bamber Bridge and a bizarre incident even by Dean Gibb's colourful standards when he was sent off in the penalty shoot-out at the end of a 4-4 draw:

> "I scored my penalty to put us 2-1 in front and I was getting some stick from the crowd so I told them to f*** off. The referee sent me off for inciting a riot but we won the shoot-out."

The FA Cup run continued with another win at the second attempt, again after a penalty shoot-out, this time against Whitby Town. Next came a tremendous 2-1 win at Stafford Rangers, who had the former Coventry City midfield player Micky Ginn in their team. Dean scored the winner and Bedlington were through to the first round proper

and a mouthwatering home tie against Colchester United from the Second Division. The build-up to the game was tremendous, with the club's press officer Bill Lowery stretched to the limit to cope with huge media interest. The Terriers' favourite restaurateur, Lassa, the Tunisian proprietor of the town's Ristorante Verdi, played his part by preparing what was to become a traditional pre-match meal before big games of soup, pasta, boiled potatoes and boiled chicken. It was the biggest game in the club's history, and Sky, BBC television and ITV were all there to supplement the usual excellent BBC Radio Newcastle coverage:

> "Colchester arrived at the ground at 1:45 and I'll never forget the look on Jason Dozzell's face. He looked at the pitch and shook his head; he was white, not black."

The ground was packed to the rafters to see Bedlington murder Colchester. Tommy Ditchburn opened the scoring off his shin to give everyone a huge lift; John Milner scored two, including a penalty, and Micky Cross got a fourth. Colchester were outplayed, outfought and overrun, and they had to be content with a late consolation goal from Tony Adcock:

> "The elation was incredible. I could have laughed and cried at the same time. That was the first of the famous all-night celebrations, with Dave and Keith and me leading the charge. We went drinking around the town and everything was for nowt. I got home at six o'clock in the morning."

The second-round draw saw Bedlington away to Scunthorpe; a tie they believed they could win, particularly if they could bring Scunthorpe back to the North-East. Sadly, it wasn't to be, and Bedlington felt with some justification that bad refereeing decisions cost them the tie. The referee missed a hand-ball in the Scunthorpe penalty area which showed up clearly on the television replays and, a minute later, awarded the home side a penalty for a challenge by Craig Melrose which at worst was robust. Scunthorpe converted the penalty and the Terriers were on their way out of the cup:

> "It was a fantastic experience and at the end the whole team ran towards our fans behind the goal and did a mass swallow dive."

It was the end of a great adventure, but there was another one lying in wait. The former Newcastle United hero Malcolm Macdonald said that Bedlington had been knocked out of the cup but they would win the FA Vase, and how close his prediction came.

Fairy tale number two of that amazing 1998-99 season began with Bedlington, who had been installed as joint favourites with Tiverton, beginning their FA Vase campaign by defeating Ramsbottom 4-1. They were leading at home to Mickleover Sports in the next round by the same score when the Welfare Park floodlights failed. Despite the best efforts of one of the linesmen, who was an electrician, the match was abandoned, and when the same thing happened the following Wednesday with Mickleover winning 3-0, the FA ordered the game to be played at Mickleover between Christmas and New Year. This time John Milner scored twice, Bedlington won 2-0 and the

Bedlington Terriers FC — 1999 FA Vase Final Squad

lights stayed on! Next, an emphatic 7-3 win over Banstead, followed by a tough tie at Dagenham against Ford, where Gibb and Milner proved to be the difference between two good sides. They inspired a 2-1 win despite the sending-off of Micky Cross.

By now Bedlington Terriers were through to the quarter-finals, where they faced their sternest test to date; a home game against Workington, who took the Terriers to extra time before Andy Bowes hit a twenty-five-yards banana shot which stuck in the stanchion and fired Bedlington into the semi-finals — excuse enough for another Perry and Gibb all-night celebration. By now Bedlington feared nobody — although they knew very little about their opponents Thame from Oxford. They would have preferred the first leg away but it wasn't to be:

> "We had them watched and were quite impressed, but we were buzzing and we really fancied our chances. Their left-back brought down Glen Renforth in the box but John Milner hit the post from the spot. We overwhelmed them though, and won the first leg 5-0."

Bedlington were virtually in the final and the hundreds who travelled south for the second leg witnessed an anti-climactic game which ended in a 0-0 draw:

> "It was a poor game but we were through to Wembley. We travelled home on Sunderland's coach and it seemed to take half-an-hour. There was everything to drink on the bus from champagne to Brown Ale. Martin Pike and I decided to travel naked but I put my clothes on later; it was a great journey."

Bedlington would play Tiverton in the final; the two favourites were through and the townspeople of Bedlington were in a mood to celebrate. The place was decked with red and white:

> "I was doing a job in Bedlington one day and people were coming out of shops and houses and shouting 'Deano, Deano.' It was fantastic."

The team had its last training session, supervised by Keith Perry and his hardworking and unsung hero of an assistant Tony Lowery, on the Wednesday before the final, then adjourned to Lassa's Ristorante Verdi for the 'last supper'. The Perry brothers were determined to do things in style and the players were told to report at Newcastle airport on Friday morning for the ten o'clock flight;

> "The pilot welcomed us aboard and wished us luck but he was a Sunderland supporter so we booed him."

The plane was met at Heathrow by the team bus with physiotherapists Derek Gair and Dave Robertson and kit-man GI Johnny on board with all the team kit. From Heathrow the coach took the team to a splendid hotel in Richmond, then it was off to Wembley for a first visit:

> "We came down the hill and saw the twin towers and I felt the hairs on the back of my neck bristle. We walked up the tunnel and I had my first glimpse of the pitch, then I walked up to the middle and kissed the centre spot. I said a prayer for my brother Neil who was 21 and I was 12 when I lost him in a motor bike accident."

The players returned to their hotel and Gibb and Milner were taken by the Perry brothers to the annual non-league dinner. When they returned John Egan was still up so Keith sent him off to bed. Egan and his fellow-goalkeeper Paul O'Connor were in the room opposite Dean and John, and that night the pair of them consumed the entire contents of the room's minibar. There was a training session the next morning at Fulham's training ground:

"O'Connor and Egan were still cockeyed. They started spewing up and they couldn't see the ball. We had shooting practice and they didn't save a shot. Keith fined the pair of them."

On Saturday night Keith Perry named his team and told the selected players they could have two pints each. Those who hadn't made the team could have anything they wanted; they included John Sokoluk who had been left out for a breach of club discipline and replaced by Andy Bowes:

"Next morning I had some orange juice, melon and grapefruit and a couple of bacon sandwiches for my breakfast then it was on the bus and off to Wembley. My hands were sweaty with the anticipation."

Ever the extrovert, Dean indulged in what was surely a Wembley first by conducting an interview with BBC Radio Newcastle during the warm-up before the kick-off:

"There was a great turn-out from the North-East. It was marvellous to see Peter Quigley and some of his players from Tow Law who had been in the

Terriers — 'Woof! Woof!'

previous year's final there to cheer us on. Roy McFarlane was the guest of honour. The game flew: I can't remember the first half although I know we had a couple of chances, but it was 0-0 at half time. It was a game of few chances; Tiverton had none and it looked like extra time, then with two minutes to go they scored with a scuffed shot which bobbled and bobbled into the corner. Everything drained away and there was total deflation. Everyone was upset and some of the players were in tears. Keith Perry couldn't accept that we had lost; I told him to look forward to next season. Anyway the crack soon started in the dressing-room. The result was a great let-down but we soon started buzzing again. We weren't going to let anything spoil our day. As we left I saw the FA Vase on their bus and I thought 'We'll win that next year.'"

There was some consolation for Bedlington in a record-breaking Northern League championship win and for Dean personally when he became the first recipient of the BBC Radio Newcastle player-of-the-year award, but dreams of a return to Wembley in 2000 were shattered by a 2-0 quarter-final replay defeat at the hands of Chippenham. Terriers retained their league title in the 1999-2000 season and played two epic Northumberland Senior Cup semi-finals against Newcastle United Reserves, but successful though the season was by any normal standards it was blighted by injury for Dean — and nothing could surpass 1998-99.

So what of the future? Eventually he'll settle down to a quiet domestic life with his wife Lisa and children Gabrielle and Ethan, but full fitness is the first priority, in readiness perhaps for one more tilt at the Vase, then we face the improbable prospect of Dean Gibb, coach and manager.

Perhaps he'll follow his mentor Keith Perry in the motivational stakes; whether it's throwing an egg on the floor and smashing it with a big hammer to symbolise crushing the opposition as he did against North Ferriby or dropping a metal weight on the dressing-room floor and hitting it so hard with the big hammer that a splinter flew off, embedded itself in his shin and caused an infection which required hospital treatment.

Whatever path Dean Gibb chooses this much is guaranteed; it won't be dull and it won't be quiet.

STAN GING

Mr. Sunday Football

Stan Ging (third from the right), with the Benton Social Club Committee,
celebrating a trophy win with Team-Captain Johnny Brecken

Stan Ging's halcyon days were spent as manager of the hugely successful Benton Social Club side in Newcastle; his success there was the culmination of a life devoted to the game of football in general and Sunday football in particular.

Stan's love of the game first manifested itself

when he was a schoolboy at Todd's Nook school off Stanhope Street in the heart of Newcastle. From there he won a scholarship to the old Rutherford College in Bath Lane, and when he left school he served his time as an apprentice fitter and turner with Vickers Armstrong's on the Tyne.

Never one to hide his light under a bushel, Stan

recalls an early brush with Norman Heaney, who lived in the Big Lamp area of the town and ran the St. Mary's Boys Club team. St. Mary's met Stan's team on the last day of the season in a match played on the Town Moor, which was a popular match venue at the time. Stan's team, which included his older brother, was leading 1-0:

> "There were no nets, and in the last minute one of their players had a shot. Heaney was standing behind the goal and he signalled to the referee that it was a goal. It was never in, but the referee accepted his word and gave a goal. 'Right', I said, 'All off!' and I marched off the field. No bugger followed me. My older brother who was playing said: 'Let the silly bugger go. You're getting dafter wor Stan.' 'Anyway,' says Norman, 'What's the difference?'

> "'Prestige,' I said. The next week I was passing the Big Lamp and I saw Norman. 'Call yourself a Catholic? You should be ashamed of yourself,' I told him. He said he'd only done it for a joke but I've never let him forget it. Every time I see I bring it up."

It would be churlish to suggest that Stan Ging was a man to harbour a grudge, but it is worth mentioning that the incident took place in 1938!

So Stan graduated to Sunday football. In fact it was he, along with Gaskell Irons, who formed the North East Sunday League in 1949 at the Green Tree pub on Scotswood Road:

> "There were some real characters involved in the Sunday League in those days. I remember 'Stagger' Wilson and Barney Moran had a fight in the dressing-room before the game once, and they were on the same team. Teams would back themselves with the bookie so there was always plenty at stake."

Stan was involved with the Green Tree team as a pacy and tricky left-winger, known variously as 'Pigeon Ging' and 'Ging on the Wing' but he moved to left-half at one stage:

> "I was known as the dirtiest half-back on the Town Moor."

Stan's departure from the Green Tree to the Royal Oak down the road took place in typical Ging circumstances. The landlord of the Green Tree had gone to the races for the day and, taking advantage of his absence, Harry Bartram went down into the cellar and switched the lines on the Bass and 'ordinary' beers so that the customers were drinking the more expensive and stronger Bass for the price of the cheaper and weaker 'ordinary'. The manager found out and barred Harry from the pub, so the entire team upped sticks and moved to the Royal Oak.

The normal routine on match days was for the team to take the number eight bus to the North Terrace pub on Claremont Road. They would change into their playing kit and hang their street clothes on the metal railings at the back of the pub, which served as their dressing room, then carry the goal-posts (no nets!) across the road onto the Town Moor and play the game. Stan went through this routine happily and successfully for many years, picking up a fractured cheekbone along the way:

> "I went up for a header and this bloke nutted me. He fractured my cheekbone. Pity; it used to be my good-looking side."

Above all. Stan Ging was, and still is, possessed of tremendous charisma, and people wanted to play for him, so when he left the Royal Oak he had no difficulty in attracting quality players. Everywhere he went in later years to watch games

Royal Oak FC

with his pal 'Big Bill' Hearne, he would point to players and say :

"He used to play for me."

And Bill would reply:

"Stan, every bugger played for you."

It has to be conceded that neither Sunday football in general nor Benton Social Club in particular were populated entirely by angelic young men. Stan's daughter Janice once asked him:

"Dad, is it true that you know all the gangsters in Newcastle?"

"Yes, they're all punchers or ladies men and some of them are both."

Among Stan's closest friends is Bobby Snowdon, who was a tremendous half-back with Benton Social Club and a man who had a fearsome reputation as Newcastle's leading hard man in the sixties and seventies.

Stan recalls one occasion when Benton were playing against the Balloon pub from the West End in a vital match. The game was played on Benton's notorious home pitch at Four Lane Ends:

"It had an oil slick on it, it was covered with dog shit and there was a path across it. Women would try to push their prams across it during games. We used to get up to 1,000 people watching. Some came for the kick-off at 11 o'clock and others stopped on their way to the pubs or the club for the 12 o'clock session. When we played the Balloon there were no nets as usual and when they claimed a goal the referee asked their manager, Bobby Reid, if it was in. Bobby said it was and the ref took his word for it. After the game I put the word about that Bobby Snowdon was looking for Reid: he vanished for days!"

That home pitch of Benton Social Club was the scene of another notable incident. It was a primitive ground in every respect; as well as the shortcomings of the playing surface, the changing facilities left a great deal to be desired. They consisted of a wooden hut which also served as a Community Centre. In the middle of the room was a snooker table where the players left their street clothes, and there were no showers. It was not uncommon for friendly neighbours to allow players to use their domestic showers to clean up after matches. Eventually, though, the Community Centre burned down and as a consequence Stan rang Lennie Cheetham (a Newcastle Blue Star stalwart in later years), who ran the Rokeby team at the time, to advise him of the position and tell him that the match would have to be cancelled:

"I told Lenny that the game was off and he said: 'Divvent be daft Stan, I'll hire a double-decker bus'. This double-decker bus turned up on the Sunday morning so Benton Social changed on the top deck and The Rokeby changed downstairs. We beat them six nowt then we all piled back on the bus and it took us all back to the club for a pint!"

That was the regular routine. After home games, both teams would return to the club for a drink, and Stan would usually end up on the stage singing:

"I was never away from the place. It was the first club in Newcastle to have strippers. Wor lass went mad because I was concert chairman at the time and she thought I would be backstage in the dressing room with the strippers."

Another great rival of Stan's was Billy Dryden, who later achieved legendary status as the Chairman of Newcastle Blue Star but who had an earlier association with a team from the Black Bull in Stanhope Street:

"I used to make Billy really mad. I always said we couldn't get a decent side out and then we would go and beat them because I worked morning, noon, and night to get a good team together. Billy used to go barmy. That bloody Ging's done it again, he used to say.

"Mind you, one of Dryden's mates at the Black Bull, Jimmy Nichol, did us a favour once. Jimmy was well known as the Newcastle United mascot but he also did a bit of refereeing and he once refereed a game of ours against The Ridges on the Town Moor. He made sure the game lasted until we scored the winner."

There was another significant 'first' in Stan's life

which involved the legendary Newcastle United centre-half of the 1950's, Frank Brennan.

Much to the annoyance of the Newcastle chairman, Stan Seymour, who owned the premier sports shop in the city, Brennan opened a rival store in Gallowgate close to St. James's Park. Stan Ging was not only Brennan's first customer but when the club, at Seymour's instigation, suspended Brennan, Stan helped to organise the public protest meetings which took place in Newcastle City Hall in support of the player.

Back to football, and a game between Benton Social Club and The Adelaide:

"There was money involved and the bets had been placed with a bookie called John Gallagher. The game was played at Nun's Moor and Gallagher was on the touch line. In those days everybody used to come to games well-dressed because they would be going to the pub afterwards. They turned out in their Crombie overcoats and silk scarves and leather gloves. Gallagher was wearing a lovely new white trench coat and he was standing on the line shouting at the referee. It was a humdinger of a game and Bobby Snowdon was in the thick of things. One thing about Bobby; you could kick him and punch him during a game and he wouldn't react, but he didn't like swearing, so when Gallagher shouted: 'Ref, you want to get

The Longbenton team Stan helped to revitilise

a hold of that dirty bastard Snowdon, he's kicking every f***** up a height' Bobby picked up two handfuls of mud and wiped them all the way down the front of Gallagher's new white coat. Gallagher vanished after that.

"I remember another time with Bobby. Incidentally, he's still my best pal. He might have done some things I didn't like in the past but he's raised thousands for charity and he's very generous. Anyway, this day we were playing out in the wilds at High Spen in County Durham. We had a bus laid on and after the game the referee asked if we would give him a lift back to Newcastle. Unfortunately my brother, who was a policeman, told Snowdon that the ref. was on the force and Bobby wouldn't let him on the bus! I pleaded with him and after the bus had gone a few hundred yards down the road he relented and let the copper on.

"I had a band of loyal players at Benton Club over the years — tough-tackling Seppy Ritson, the brothers Kenny and Jackie Best, John Brecken (who captained the team for many years), goalkeeper Billy Patrick, midfield-general Brian Mallen, Eddie Bell and Wila Doyle. All good players and good lads."

Sadly, after 15 happy years at Benton Social Club, Stan left in acrimonious circumstances. At a presentation night which otherwise had been highly successful a member of the football committee accused Stan of thinking he was the only one who did any work:

"OK. If that's the way you feel, run it yourselves."

was Stan's response, and he moved on. He had a three-year stint at The Runnymede in Westerhope, where he recruited excellent players of the calibre of Peter Flaherty, Tommy Dixon, Jimmy

McFarlane, Rob Willis, Kenny Best and Vic Hillier ('a lovely lad, but what a dirty bugger').

It wasn't the same, however, and Stan left and had a spell away from the game. He returned to help Longbenton FC, who were struggling, after a cry for help from Jimmy Fawcett Snr:

"I enjoyed it there. One of the best things was a lot of the lads who were with me at Longbenton later made a success of non-league management: the likes of Dave Beynon and Bob Morton were first class."

It was at Benton Social Club, though, that Stan Ging's star shone brightest:

"I loved it there. I remember when two of the team got themselves barred from Benton Club so they went along the road and signed for the Black Bull. I loved going in there and winding them up by saying: 'How did Benton reserves do today?'"

Stan's involvement was total. His passion for the game was open and apparent, not least when he was on the line encouraging his own team:

"There were no track suits then. Top coat and gloves. My gloves spent more time on the ground than they did on my hands. Whenever a player missed a pass or a tackle or shot off target I would throw my gloves on the ground in frustration. They even used to end up in the trainer's water bucket. I don't know how I didn't have a heart attack. I think as many people turned up to watch my antics as came to see the games."

One of Stan's former players, and favourite, the late Albert Denholm, summed up his tremendous passion and commitment:

"It was pissing down with rain one day and there

was only one mad bugger running up and down shouting the odds — Stan! That's why I played for him on that horrible pitch. He loved the game and everybody loved him."

Stan's most often-used phrase is 'he's a very good friend of mine', which he applies with regard to players at every level. Geordie Carrick from The Rocket pub in Longbenton once decided to put Stan's claims to the test. The occasion was the Inter Cities Fairs Cup tie between Rangers and Newcastle United at Ibrox Park in 1969. Stan and a bunch of regulars from The Rocket had travelled up to Glasgow for the game and were standing outside the ground when the coach

carrying the Newcastle team pulled up. As the players emerged Geordie Carrick saw his opportunity and challenged Stan:

"There's Bobby Moncur. He's a very good friend of yours isn't he Stan? Let's go across."

Over they went and when the Newcastle captain spotted Stan he said:

"Hello Stan; great to see you. That was a smashing night last week. Thanks a million."

That was Geordie put firmly in his place and Stan's claim to have 'very good friends' at every level in the game amply confirmed.

Stan (far right) with Longbenton after winning the League Cup at Heaton Stannington

These days, Stan is a member of the Executive Committee of Bedlington Terriers Football Club, albeit in a low-key and advisory capacity. He still travels to matches in the company of 'Big Bill' Hearne, his tall and very quiet pal. It's a combination which prompted Ian Crumplin to dub Stan 'Don Corleone', which is quite appropriate for a man who once 'knew all the gangsters in Newcastle'. Appropriate, too, because Stan regarded all his players as his family and his loyalty was unswerving.

They say that Geordies are born with football in their blood and in Stan Ging's case that is manifestly true. He may be in the autumn of his years but 'Pigeon' Ging, the man they remember as Mr. Sunday Football, has lost none of his passion.

'Stan the Man!'

JOE JABS

The Harrogate Kid and a drop of sherry

'Joe at the ready'

Joe Jabs has been the physiotherapist at Whitley Bay Football Club for the past 20 years and he is a man who has grown into a job. One afternoon in the late seventies Joe, who is a painter and decorator by trade, was sitting in his local club playing dominoes, as was his regular habit, when he was assailed by the thought that there was more to life. His good friend Micky Fairley responded to Joe's observation by inviting him to go and watch a football match. Micky played for Howdon

British Legion and Joe went along. He enjoyed the game and was indulging in his customary pint afterwards when he was approached by the team manager, Joe Fisher, and asked if he would be interested in becoming the team's 'sponge man'. Armed only with his new-found interest and enthusiasm and devoid of any of the requisite knowledge, Joe accepted:

> "My first game this player went down and I sprinted on. I was in a total panic. The referee asked me what the problem was and I had to say 'He's just taken a bit of a knock.' I hadn't a clue."

After that the club paid for him to go on a first aid course with the St. John's Ambulance Brigade, and Joe's fledgling career began to take off. He knew Jimmy Florence who was the physio at North Shields FC at the time, and he asked Florence if he could watch and learn from him. Once he was reassured that Joe held a basic first aid certificate Jimmy agreed, and the manager, Peter Flaherty, had no objection as long as Joe didn't get in the way.

At first Joe just watched and absorbed knowledge, and he gradually picked up the basics of the job:

> "I went as a model on a sports injury course and we began to take the course around schools; that was how I learned to spot and diagnose injuries and to be able to treat and strap them. One Saturday after I had been at Shields for three years as Jimmy Florence's number two I was told 'you're in charge', but although I knew a reasonable amount by then, I still wasn't fully competent, to be honest."

A change in management at North Shields saw Peter Flaherty leave and the partnership of Jim Pearson and Bobby Elwell took over. In Joe's view there was no real chemistry between the two newcomers and he felt the time had come to move on. Coincidentally, he received a telephone call from Tommy Moody who was the Secretary at Whitley Bay, where there was a vacancy for a physio. Jimmy Florence had recommended Joe for the job and they were anxious to know if he was interested:

> "I was like a little kid. It was just as if the manager of England was ringing me up. I went along to Hillheads for an interview and I was a bag of nerves. Alan Moore the milkman was the chairman and I met him and the committee, who said the job was looking after the first team. I panicked when they said that but I agreed to take the job until they found someone better; that was 17 years ago and I think they paid me a fiver a week. I was lucky because when I walked into the dressing room the first person I saw was Paul Dixon, who made me very welcome. He said, 'it's about time we had you here', and that made me feel good. I must admit I was on an ego-trip but I was still nervous because I was working on my own and I had all the responsibility. I still didn't know enough on the medical side. For instance Ian Chandler, the centre-forward, had a lump in his groin and I didn't know what it was; I do now — it was a haematoma — but I didn't then. Chandler asked me what it was and I had to be honest and admit my ignorance. I don't think it did my credibility in the dressing-room much good."

The biggest shock Joe received when he took over at Hillheads related to the lack of treatment equipment. At North Shields he had worked with top-class equipment in a dedicated treatment room which even had an ultrasonic machine. Whitley Bay's equipment consisted of one heat-lamp:

> "They used that heat-lamp for everything from heart transplants to treating verrucas."

Whitley Bay FC before winning the Northumberland Senior Cup at St. James's Park

In those early days Joe needed permission from the chairman on a match-to-match basis to buy basic equipment and medical supplies. He was allowed to open an account with Potts the Chemists: Mr Potts was a club director and Joe used to go down to the shop on Saturday mornings and fill a bag with the necessary oils, deep-heat rubs and bandages:

"One day I came to the ground with an empty bag. They wouldn't serve me because the account was overdue. The players went mad. 'Call yourself a physio', they said but I said, 'don't blame me, blame the ******* chairman; he's not paying the bills.' That afternoon I ran onto the field with an empty bag just to look the part but I had no credibility. We lived like that, hand-to-mouth, for years in the Northern League. We always survived but had no real success; it wasn't surprising, really."

Managers came and went in Joe's early years at Hillheads. Former Scottish international John Connolly came as player/manager and Joe recalls him spending 15 minutes before his first game telling the players in no uncertain terms that he would not tolerate foul and abusive language and then being red-carded 30 seconds into the game for swearing at the referee.

When Bobby Graham and Paul Dixon took over the reins of management there was an immediate and positive change in the atmosphere at the club:

"The whole place began to generate. With Alan Lingwood as chairman and Billy Rogerson, Charlie Davis, Stan Rutter and Gordon Crawford on the board there was a desire for success within the club. We reached the final of the Northumberland Senior Cup and played

Peter Robinson puts Whitley Bay ahead in the FA Cup against Preston, before the 'Match of the Day' cameras

Blue Star at St James's Park. It was like going to Wembley. I remember sitting in the dug-out, and running out onto the park. My trademark has always been to get to the injured player as fast as possible: I tried to be like a greyhound out of the traps. The players called me the fastest physio in the west, but it was just the excitement. I loved to go on because I was part of the day. It was like being an actor in a theatre and there was no bigger stage than St. James's Park."

Joe's pre-match routine in the dressing room is the stuff of legend, dashing around handing out tie-ups and chewing-gum, giving players rubs:

"I tried to do the best I could; I was always haunted by the fear that I would lose my job. I was terrified of that because I was so proud. By three o'clock I was exhausted through giving the players rubs. The sweat used to pour out of me, but it had to be done right. Then you're in the dug-out and you've got to be ready. After Bobby Graham's first year the club brought in top-class players like Kevin Todd, Paul Walker and Tony Harrison, and when they first came it was a bit intimidating. I was a bit in awe of them. It was in my mind that I would look a plonker but once I got to know them it was no problem."

1989 was probably the greatest year in the entire history of Whitley Bay Football Club and Joe was an integral part of the success. He was so confident of the team's ability that when the opposition took the field he sat in his dug-out watching them and wondering how many goals Whitley would beat them by.

Whitley Bay reached the first round proper of the

Celebrating in style after beating Preston

FA Cup by defeating Southport 2-0 and were then drawn away to Scarborough. When Kevin Todd kicked a football against a mirror in the dressing room before kick-off Joe's superstitious nature caused him to fear the worst, but instead of seven years' bad luck Bay scored a late winner to book their place in the second round and a memorable home tie against Preston North End:

"I was delighted with the Scarborough result and I was confident we could beat Preston. It was an unforgettable day. There were thousands in the ground including the great Tom Finney. When we went 1-0 up I thought we would win and when we made it 2-0 I bloody knew we would win. 'Match of the Day' that night showed 20 minutes of the game and John Motson gave me a mention. That was a big moment. I remember the game vividly but I can't remember how drunk I was afterwards. Then we drew Rochdale away in the third round. We would have beaten any team at home, and even away from home everybody was up for it."

Bobby Graham changed his goalkeeper for the Rochdale game and Joe remembers the players being taken aback by the decision. When Rochdale took the lead Whitley never recovered; the game was lost, the great adventure was over, and Joe endured one of the most disappointing days of his life. Whitley Bay actually finished that season without winning any silverware but the memories remain untarnished.

Having taken advantage of the pyramid system which was in operation, Whitley had progressed from the Northern League to the HFS Loans League, where they were competing successfully:

"We had to go to Wales as well as places like Liverpool, Manchester, Sheffield and Leeds. It was an adventure. Once we were travelling back and the bus broke down at Harrogate just 100 yards from a pub. When we were told it would take two or three hours for a replacement bus to arrive a great cheer went up and we all went to the pub. There was a band on and I liked a dance. I'd had a good drink and when this woman asked me up I was game. We started dancing then we had a bit of a smooch. I started taking her gear off on the dance floor and her mates were shouting at her, 'stop it you dirty cow.' I told her to take no notice, and our chairman Alan Lingwood apologised to the pub

manager, but he was standing on a crate to get a better view and said it was the best night they had ever had. They wanted to book me for the next week and the lads had a whip-round on the bus on the way home. The called me the Harrogate Kid and when I told the wife about it she said I should write a book with all the lies I told."

When the team travelled to Wales they normally played on Saturday and Sunday, travelling down on Friday night. The players stayed in the hotel but Joe and the club secretary Rob Harding went out drinking. When Joe returned he was so drunk he had to be carried to bed, and he was still drunk the next day, to the extent that the manager wouldn't let him treat the players.

On another week-end away Joe once again ended up worse for wear:

"I couldn't see the players and when one of them was hurt I ran on the pitch and the referee had to show me where he was. Instead of treating him I tried to give him a drink of sherry from a bottle I had in my bag. The last game of the season was at Eastwood Town and everyone was demob happy. There was a bin in the middle of the dressing room and Billy Johnson had a shit in it. We were in great fettle because we had won the league, and on the way back the players held me out of the bus skylight; we were travelling at about 70 miles an hour and the plan was to climb along the roof and back into the bus through the door. They had second thoughts and pulled me back in; I looked like Worzel Gummidge and my face looked like a car bumper covered with midges."

During the close season Dave Ashton, a qualified physio, joined the club to help Joe and they quickly became firm friends and drinking companions. The arrangement seemed to be that

Joe taught Dave about drinking and Dave taught Joe about medical matters. Things didn't always go smoothly and on one occasion Dave was left behind in Wales, but Joe usually managed to play his part by organising a bottle of sherry and several cans of beer for the journey home.

The club was buzzing at that time and there were some real characters on the playing side — none more than Billy Lees, Perry Briggs and his big pal, John Carver (now with Newcastle United).

On another unforgettable journey home, this time from Barrow, the team bus collided with a cow:

> "It was a dark Saturday night and at about 7:15 there was a screech of brakes and a tremendous thump, and there was this dead cow in the road. We were half pissed and we couldn't shift it but we were just outside this country pub so we went in. They had heard the commotion and they weren't very pleased, so when we went in chanting 'Toon Army' and Billy Johnson asked for 15 beef sandwiches, the landlord went berserk and called us murderers. One of the players phoned his girl-friend; they had just got back together but when he told her he would be late back because there was a dead cow blocking the road she said he was a liar and just wanted to stay out drinking with his mates, and she finished with him."

One of Joe's happiest memories underlines the camaraderie which is an integral feature of non-league football. The team went to Leek Town with a 4-0 first leg advantage in the league cup final but they lost the away leg 1-0 to win the cup 4-1 on aggregate. They stayed on afterwards for a drink and the Leek people laid on a magnificent buffet for the Whitely Bay party and lined the street to applaud them when they left. It wouldn't happen in the Premiership.

Joe is still very much a part of the Hillheads scene, combining his physiotherapy duties with his day job, painting and decorating.

Joe is a died-in-the-wool Whitley Bay man who has been with the club for 20 years and once turned down 'serious money' to go to Gateshead. The club has no spare money so Joe is paid in a rather unorthodox way:

> "I once told the chairman I should get a glass of sherry every time I ran onto the pitch. At last season's presentation night there were two litres of sherry for me. Mind you, I had them drunk before I got home in the taxi. After one away game when the programme notes said I got withdrawal symptoms if I didn't get a bottle of sherry, their supporters club presented me with a bottle."

Joe also remembers one of the best presentation nights he attended at Whitley. Paul Ferris, now physio at Newcastle United, along with Pete Embelton, gave a 50-minute show mimicking directors, players, physios, and supporters. They were absolutely brilliant.

Joe's present emotions are those of disappointment. He feels sympathy for a capable manager who until a recent influx of new directors has had no money to spend, and as far as his own ambitions are concerned he hopes to beat Jimmy Florence's record of 18 years as club physio:

> "I hope my little legs will keep me going and I can stay sober enough to recognise the players when I run out to treat them."

Joe's legendary status at Whitley Bay is guaranteed. He has a personalised seat in the dug-out, and the seat and its occupant are firm fixtures at Hillheads. He also enjoys a bottle of

Joe enjoys his favourite tipple

Brown Ale in the corner of the bar with the old brigade of supporters; Sid Cope, Cockney Roger, Tommy Moody and Lyn Bone.

One final point; it will not have been lost on the discerning reader that Jabs is a singularly appropriate name for a physiotherapist. To be strictly accurate Jabs is not Joe's given name; his actual surname is Jabanowski, but the story of the metamorphosis into Jabs is a complicated one involving a Russian grandfather, a Polish grandmother who couldn't pronounce Jabanowski and an American father. If you're really interested in the complexities of Joe's family tree, buy a bottle of sherry, make your way to Hillheads on match day and ask him yourself!

FRANK LAW

Denis Law's brother and Malcolm Allison

Frank with Malcolm Allison

Frank Law comes from a footballing family. His father Alec managed the Innisfree Catholic Club team, and Frank and his brother Graham were both fearless and very capable centre-forwards; the only member of the family who didn't play football was his brother Denis, who was named after a football legend!

It was while he was playing for the Innisfree alongside his brother that Frank sustained the injury which hastened the end of his career at the age of 24 and caused him to follow his father into management. The injury was caused by the sort of straightforward collision which every striker experiences; he lunges for the ball which ends up in the back of the net ahead of the goalkeeper's despairing dive and the keeper lands on the forward's leg. The consequence was knee ligament damage which even the healing skills of the legendary Harold Burgess, the 'Fenham magician', couldn't heal. Harold had a remarkable gift, and players from all levels in the game, including professionals whose clubs were not aware of their visits, came to him for help:

"He really was a magician and his fingers got straight to the spot. I was lying on a bench while he worked on my knee. He had a milk bottle behind it and he was putting me through agony while his whippet sat alongside me grinning. To be fair to Harold he did get me some movement back, but the knee wouldn't stand up to playing: it was never the same. Ian Playfair was running North Heaton Sports Club at the time and he asked me to sign for them. I signed the form but really the knee was gone and I only signed to help him out if he had an emergency.

"I didn't want to play but towards the end of the season there was a message on the answering machine saying 'I'll pick you up tomorrow'. It was ridiculous. I was bad with the drink from the night before and I hadn't played a game all season. When Ian's car pulled up at the house I told him I didn't have any boots but he said he'd find me a pair.

"The game was at Wallsend Rising Sun ground against Westerhope Hillheads, who needed to win to take the title. When we got to the ground there were whippets running round the track. Both sides were pumped up for the game and there was no love lost. The first time I was tackled I went down like a rag doll and there

were feet flying everywhere and players going down like bags of hammers. It was like a scene from M.A.S.H. Mick Colwill wiped out their centre-half, who was a huge bloke, with one tackle, then when the two of them were going back from a corner Mick hit him with a short-arm jab. He was stretched out on the pitch and they needed smelling salts to bring him round. I asked Mick what had happened and he said the bloke had told him he had 'done' Mick in a game five years earlier. Mick said, 'he shouldn't have jogged my memory!' Anyway, we drew 2-2 and did them for the league title."

Frank did go on to play a season for the Victory pub in South Gosforth for his pal Billy Moreland, but the knee couldn't cope and Frank's love of a pint meant that he was overweight into the bargain, so the following season he began to help Billy out on the non-playing side — and it was thus that his career in management began.

The Victory is a small pub in a Newcastle suburb, and their team played in the lowest division of the North East Sunday League, but when Frank joined Billy Moreland in running the team they had the nucleus of a good, young, pacy side and with the pair of them in partnership, assisted by a great supporter and committee member Norman Walmsley who looked after the finances, the team moved inexorably through the leagues from lowly 'K' Division to Division 'B', with most of the players remaining in the side throughout that successful six-year period. So what was the secret of Frank Law's success?

"I could motivate. That was the key. I used to do a mile of work picking players up, dropping them off, wiping their backsides, and they appreciated it. They would run through brick walls for me. We won five league championships and played in three cup finals in six years and we did the double three times,

Victory for 'The Victory'

and after every game we went back to the Victory and had a real good drink."

When you hear Frank Law talking about that highly impressive record the realisation dawns on you that this is not a brash, in-your-face football manager with a big ego. He was certainly committed, and his touchline histrionics were comparable with the best, but when he reflects on those glory days he talks not about himself but about the players in whom he engendered such loyalty and devotion. No player earned higher admiration in Frank's eyes than his centre-half Keith Muckle:

"Keith was amazing. He played for me for 11 seasons without missing a game of any sort; that's over 300 games and he was never booked, which is incredible for a centre-half. He could have been anything and everything in the game if the chance had come his way. He went to the same school as Peter Beardsley but he never got a league club even though he was a class player. For sheer consistency he was phenomenal and his dedication was amazing; he just wouldn't miss a game. After one game around Christmas time he came off limping with a groin problem. He had a lump the size of a cricket ball in his groin area and when I asked him about it he said he had been struggling with it for six weeks, but he wouldn't miss a game and he played until the end of the season as well as playing for Alnwick Town on a Saturday."

On another occasion Frank went to pick up Keith from his house for a match, and when Keith climbed into the car he was clearly in some distress. When the game kicked off the opposition played a high ball into the penalty area and Keith jumped and headed it away, then went down on his knees grimacing with pain. Shortly afterwards the same thing happened and again he was doubled up in agony after heading the ball clear. It transpired that he had been playing with three broken ribs, and when Frank asked him about it he shrugged his shoulders and said:

"They can't do anything for you. You've just got to get on with it!"

This philosophy was probably the product of a life which had contained its fair share of health problems. At the age of 14 Keith was diagnosed as having an infected kidney and he underwent a major kidney operation. The kidney caused him periodic problems and one season it was particularly troublesome, requiring him to attend hospital for tests. It turned out that his other kidney was infected and the hospital's message was a stark one: have the kidney removed or die. He was booked into Freeman Hospital for a kidney operation, but the day he was due for admission coincided with a cup quarter-final tie against the Balloon, so Keith told the hospital it was his daughter's birthday and they agreed to put back his admission time from ten in the morning until six o'clock the same night. He played in the match, scored the winning goal and went back to the Victory for the usual post-match drink. Frank dropped him off at the hospital at six o'clock — when he had his pre-operative tests. Two hours later he was in the Brandling pub in South Gosforth; he had eight pints and a kebab and returned to the hospital at 11:15pm. He had his kidney removed on the Monday morning and when Frank visited him that evening his wound was stapled together with metal staples. The following week's match was called off and the week after Keith turned up with his boots expecting to play:

"He still had the staples in and I wouldn't even think of letting him play. He called me all the bastards but if I'd let him play his insides would have been on the pitch."

One particular performance of Keith Muckle's was described by the former Newcastle United and Middlesbrough defender Irving Nattrass as the most complete he had ever seen from anyone in any class of football. It was a Sunday League 'B' Division match between the Victory and Saltwell which was crunch game, as the Victory needed to win that match and the next to win the league. They played on a tight pitch at Redheugh in Gateshead and Saltwell played three centre-forwards; their strategy was simple — everyone including the goalkeeper humped high balls forward for the front three, but Keith won literally everything, then went upfield for two corners and scored the goals which won the game. Some player.

One of Frank Law's many attributes was his unstinting willingness to work hard, and as a result of his fundraising activities end-of-season trips for the Victory players to places like Blackpool, Southport and the Isle of Man became regular events. One year a party of 30 players and officials set off for Blackpool. Frank had raised £3500, and as well as paying for the coach and the accommodation he was able to provide each player with £100 spending money. The coach departed from the Victory:

"Everything was paid for, even the beer and the stottie sandwiches on the coach. We got on the bus after a few pints in the Victory and some of the lads started playing cards. My brother Graham and his mates, Denny Quinn and Larry Moat, were wicked card players and one or two of the lads had lost their money before we crossed the Tyne Bridge. One of them was totally skint and we had to have a whip-round for him when we got to Blackpool. Some of the lads were drinking and playing cards all the way to Blackpool but we had made a rule that all cards had to stop when Blackpool Tower came into sight. As we drove into Blackpool the lads carried on playing cards under their seats so they couldn't see the Tower. Most of us fell off the bus into the hotel. Those trips were something else; we were just like a big family. Mind, one time we finished up in Liverpool Crown Court. We were in a club in Southport having a quiet drink when a fight broke out. We weren't involved but one of them hit a player with a baseball bat. The place erupted but I grabbed the bouncer and handed him over when the police arrived and we ended up in court giving evidence against him."

Young manager with his hands full

Successful football teams are usually adept in the art of celebration and the Victory were no exception. One season they won a cup final at the nearby Heaton Stannington ground in High Heaton but unfortunately there was a new manager in the Victory who was less enthusiastic about the football team than his predecessor had been, and he made it clear that there would be no after-hours celebrations if the team won the cup. Consequently, Frank had booked the function suite at the now-defunct Gosforth greyhound stadium, where the proprietor had promised a showing of blue movies to go alongside the buffet and bar. The celebrations of the cup win were carried out in professional style:

"We were full of drink and we were having races down the straight of the dog track with money changing hands. What a day."

The change in management at the Victory brought about a change in Frank's own allegiances. The previous manager had been a very keen supporter but the change in landlord brought about a decline both in enthusiasm for the team and in the fortunes of the pub itself. Frank had been drinking in the Killingworth Arms in Killingworth village two or three miles away and when the manager there, Ken Hodgson, expressed an interest, Frank moved the team lock, stock and barrel to Killingworth.

Success was more difficult to attain and sustain as the team was already well established and playing to a high standard in the North East Sunday League 'B' Division, but Frank Law set high standards, and with a side which included Craig Melrose and Mark Cameron, both members of the 1999 Bedlington Terriers FA Vase Finalists side, and encouraged by an extremely supportive pub manager and clientele, he took his new team to promotion to the Premier Division of the

Sunday League. Celebrations were undiminished from the Victory days and it was like New Year's Eve every Sunday at the Killingworth Arms, with Frank at the centre of events with his renditions of Lindisfarne's 'Meet Me on the Corner' and Leo Sayer's 'One Man Band'. Pub landlord Ken Hodgson demonstrated his support by twice paying the £500 required for a season's pitch hire:

"He was a businessman and he was no mug. He knew how much we spent in his pub. Once, we had a day at Newcastle races and went back to the pub afterwards. We were there until three in the morning; you needed a sick note to go home at eleven o'clock. Many a Sunday night we just sent out for an Indian or Chinese takeaway and carried on drinking.

"I remember once we were playing the Balloon away in the cup. They were a cracking team and most of our lads were unknown but I was so convinced we would win that I said I would shave my 'tash' off if we beat them. They were a top team and on paper we didn't have a chance, but we beat them 1-0. I'd grown that 'tash' since I was 17 but that day I shaved it off in the lounge of the 'Killie' Arms in front of everybody. I shaved half of it off first and went on a lap of honour, then I finished the job. When I got home the wife never even noticed!"

It was in 1995 that Frank's managerial skills with the Killingworth Arms came to the attention of the media in the shape of the Tyne Tees Television company. Ian Lennox and Bob Whittaker from Tyne Tees were looking for a Sunday team which could benefit from some professional coaching imput; the plan was to monitor the team's progress and produce a documentary programme for TV transmission. The considerable coaching talents of Malcolm Allison, the former Manchester City coach, Lennie Heppell, the internationally respected balance expert, and Steve Black, the fitness guru with Newcastle Falcons rugby union club and latterly the Welsh national side were recruited:

"Allison concentrated mostly on the ball and he was particularly effective defensively; Lennie was the balance expert and Blackie looked after the fitness side. They took the training twice a week and they certainly changed the players' awareness and Blackie improved their fitness levels. I wasn't inhibited one bit. They came in the dressing room and the cameras were at half of our games but I was the manager and I was in charge. The lads enjoyed the experience and we didn't win the league but we did finish fifth, playing good football. I couldn't really see how they could make a film of it all but I was impressed with what they did."

Among the more entertaining scenes in the finished version of the 'Just For Kicks' documentary were those showing Frank on the touchline wearing his trademark cap and berating players and officials alike:

"It was a drug. I was totally involved. I had a dodgy watch, by the way, which slowed down when we were winning and speeded up when we were losing!"

That television experience marked five years of management at the Killingworth Arms for Frank Law, and he decided it was an appropriate moment to bow out:

"The time had been reached when I had to consider my wife and two kids. Women have a lot to put up with. I worked hard all week as a painter and decorator and I knew I should have been spending the weekends with the family. I loved the football. I was a winner who wanted to win, but you've got to be responsible.

Killingworth Arms FC

Besides, you can only say the same things to the same players so many times: I wasn't a coach, I was a manager. To have had three major coaches in the dressing room with Frank Law as the manager was a great accolade so I felt it was right that the television season should be my last. I called it a day and I admit I was crying when the time came. The start of the next season was hard, but I quickly got over it."

A lifelong Newcastle United supporter and a season-ticket holder of five years standing, he has devoted his time to watching them, and when he has felt passionately about issues surrounding the club he has expressed his views coherently in letters to the local press. It is a source of considerable pride that of the seven letters Frank has written to the local football paper, five have won £25 'best letter' prizes.

Nowadays you'll find Frank and his brother

Graham enjoying a weekend pint in the Ship on Newcastle's Old Coast Road, talking football and reminiscing. One topic which is sure to come up is Frank's amazing record of success at Northumberland FA disciplinary hearings in defence of his players:

"Nobody wins appeals, but I won three out of three. They used to call me Perry Mason. One lad was charged with butting an opponent but I just told them he was a nice lad and he wouldn't do that. I said if he had he would never play for me again. I told no lies, just the truth, and they believed me."

Frank is proud of the fact that at both the Victory and the Killingworth Arms his teams played good football and never indulged in kicking opponents:

"I was aggressive and mad on the line but the good

Frank with his brother Graham

name of the team was important. I wore a sheepskin coat and a cap and I looked like a spiv but I kicked every ball. The players grew up with me and we had a great affinity. We would do anything for each other; that was the secret. I spent hours flying around collecting them from birds' houses all over the place, then they'd come and play blinders for me."

After 11 devoted years Frank received a silver salver in grateful recognition of his efforts, and he is entirely without regrets. So a man from the footballing family who at 16 was himself considered a genuine prospect but who in his own judgement left junior football a year early to play for his dad's team, a man who learned the fundamentals of management from his father and whose mother and wife both washed team strips every week, now enjoys a family life and appreciates it:

"Gloria knew the score; she's an absolute diamond. I've been lucky, but I've always played the game by her."

Frank Law is that kind of bloke. He loved his football and his players, he values his family and he is quick and generous in his praise of others, but he can watch his video of 'Just For Kicks' and look at his silver salver secure in the knowledge that his considerable efforts were recognised and appreciated.

JACKIE MARKS

Blyth Spartans, the FA Cup, and a sandwich-filling.

'That fateful night at St. James Park'

The high point of the Jackie Marks story is the stuff of fable; guiding a non-league football team to the fifth round of the FA Cup and to within a whisker of a tie against mighty Arsenal.

More of that later, but the first impact Jack made on the game was as a 16-year-old player representing Dudley in the old Miners Welfare League before completing his junior career, in which he was a goalscoring inside-forward, in the colours of Seaton Burn Juniors:

"I was a skilful player, but in those days we could all trap a ball, head a ball and pass a ball. Now if they can do those things they are internationals."

Jack's early success attracted the attention of Newcastle United, who ran five sides then and were always on the lookout for local talent:

"I was 19 and I went along on Tuesday and Thursday nights but there were a lot of lads there and it was a bit chaotic. I did play a couple of games for the reserves and a few for the third team but there wasn't a lot of interest showed and I signed for Shankhouse."

National Service intervened and like many more Jack was called up to serve in the army, an experience which had a maturing effect on the young man from Burradon:

"It was like a comedy film at first. You got the train, reported to the camp, went through a door into a hut and had your hair cut, then through another door where they stuck six needles in you, but once things settled down it was the making of me. I was posted overseas and I captained the British Army team in Japan when I was on leave. Not that I was the best player in the army; the best players didn't get posted! I also spent a fortnight at battle school where all the ammunition was live, and I visited Hiroshima. They were tough experiences and by the time I got back to England I'd had enough of the army. I said I wouldn't salute another officer, so they sent me on an exercise to Salisbury Plain for the last three weeks of my time to keep me out of the way. I was always honest and the army made me a strong character."

After the army it was back to Burradon, and just one week after his demobilisation Jack married Hazel, his schooldays sweetheart:

"We met when I was 15 at High Pit pictures and we were engaged before I joined up. I came out of the army with £10, got married, found a job then looked around for somewhere to play football."

The solution came in the shape of Newburn FC in the Northern Alliance, a strong team in a strong league. The Newburn side included Tommy Bolam the captain, who was a former professional, as well as Eddie Watts, a tough-tackling full-back, and Jimmy Rankin who had played for Grimsby Town:

"We played Blyth once in the Northumberland Senior Cup and they had the ex-Middlesbrough winger Billy Linacre playing for them. Tommy Bolam told us to put him in the stand as soon as he got the ball, so Eddie Watts clipped him a couple of times and I hit him with a hard tackle, then he didn't want to know."

Football at local level attracted good crowds at the time, and in 1957 25,000 turned out to watch Jack and his brother Albert play for Newburn against Ashington in the Senior Cup final at St James' Park:

"I had a bit of an injury so I went to see this bloke in Lemington and he said I had a twisted hamstring. I didn't know what he meant; I thought it was a sandwich-filling."

Newburn, who also had Peter Feenan's father in their ranks, lost the game 2-1 but the following week they gained revenge by beating them 3-1 in the final of the Northern Alliance Challenge Cup, which was a notable achievement as Ashington was a professional club at the time.

During that spell with Newburn Jack turned down opportunities to join Stockport County and Workington, and after a short spell elsewhere he returned to combine Saturday football with Newburn and Sunday games for the Red Lion pub in Shieldfield:

"The Red Lion team was managed by John Henderson and run from a pub managed by Ginger Roberts, the ex-boxer. Dickie Robson played for West Brom Reserves on Saturdays and the Red Lion on Sundays. I was their leading goalscorer one season from centre-half; I scored a load from free-kicks and penalties."

Jack was by now in his late thirties and beginning to turn his attention away from the playing side of the game towards coaching. His final fling as a player came when he went with a friend who was having a trial for Ponteland United. The team was managed by Booby Cowell, who won three FA Cup winners' medals with Newcastle United in the 1950's, and Jack turned out because they were short of players. He stayed for the whole season, scoring 34 goals as a centre-forward before hanging up his boots and taking his coaching badges. Alan Brown and Stan Calvert, coaching gurus at Newcastle University, took him through his preliminary badges before he completed his full badge at Houghall College in Durham.

He began by coaching for the Northumberland FA before accepting his first team-coaching appointment with Gosforth and Coxlodge in the Northern Alliance:

Jackie (back, fourth from the left) qualifying as an FA Coach at Houghill College, Durham

Early days at Croft Park (Jackie, standing at far right)

"They were a decent side with players like Tommy Handysides, Harry Powell, Graham Sanderson and Alan Wilson, and it was there that the first seeds were sown."

Blyth Spartans were going through a difficult spell, and their chairman Bob Middleton invited Jack to be interviewed for a job there. He was interviewed by 20 committee members, who then appointed Tony Knox as manager!

"I was working at Winthrop Laboratories and one day Jimmy Turney, who virtually ran Blyth Spartans, came to see me at work. Tony Knox had quit after six months in charge and they asked me to take over, which I did."

That was in the 1967-68 season, and the team finished fifth in the league. The basis of a good side was there and Jack built on it by bringing in players of the calibre of Ronnie Scott, Michael Hind, Des Jardine, Eddie Alder, Brian Slane and Gordon Scott — all quality players. Things progressed well for the next two seasons until there was a falling out between Jack and Jimmy Turney:

"When I took the job in the first place I did so on the basis that I didn't want any money until I had proved myself, and I accepted ten shillings a week. After a couple of seasons I felt justified in asking if it could be reviewed; I was out of pocket, what with scouting and travelling, and we were top of the league with four games to play. Turney said I might as well leave straight away because I had done nowt for the club! I made him come into the dressing room and repeat what he had told me in front of the players. They were in revolt and Turney tried all ways to make amends but I stuck to my guns. My pride was involved. I had taken them from the bottom and the next season they reached the semi-final of the Amateur Cup."

Jack's next club was Tow Law Town, where he was recruited by Chairman Harry Hodgson and Secretary Bernard Fairbairn, and he again proved his capabilities by taking them to the quarter-finals of the FA Amateur Cup. Very good players including Tommy Pickford, Dickie Longstaff, Jimmy Leach and Terry Hunt played in a side which met Skelmersdale United in the quarter-final. The Lancashire side included Steve

Heighway, who went on to stardom with Liverpool, and Micky Burns whose career included a very successful spell at Newcastle United. Tow Law lost 1-0 to a side which scored four in the semi-final and five in the final to win the trophy. Jack, though, was not entirely convinced of Tow Law's ambition and Spennymoor United were looking for a manager. John Smith and Stan Bradley ran the show and they offered Jack the job, but in the meantime Ken Prior was appointed as Ashington's manager and wanted Jack as his coach:

"I thought it might be a bit too cosy at Spennymoor as they were a very successful side while Ashington were poor, so I decided to go there. Things went badly at first and I thought I might have to leave, but towards the end of the season Ken Prior gave up and I was put in charge, and that was when the fun started."

Within a season-and-a-half Jack had brought a group of very talented footballers to Portland Park: Michael Ritchie, Billy Scott, Billy Blair, Les Mutrie, Vin Pearson, plus a young goalscorer from Craster called Brian Pringle and the old warhorse from Whitley Bay, Billy Wright:

"Billy was the icing on the cake. Things weren't going well for him at Whitley and I told him if he signed for me he would never be out of the team. He was the leader and in my second season we reached the semi-final of the Amateur Cup."

The cup run began in the extra preliminary round and ended in the last semi-final ever of the competition: Ashington were one game away from being the only team to have played in every round:

"We had two great games against Slough. They had been in the final the previous year and they thought they were going to win it. The manager of the Holiday Inn down there invited us for free food and drink as a gesture of goodwill, but the players were so greedy he had to close the bar and stop the food after 20 minutes! We drew down there and when we found out that we were 7-1 to win the replay we sent this kid to the bookies with the money to bet on ourselves. We won 1-0 and the Slough players didn't like it. They were starting to work themselves up in the clubhouse afterwards but that soon stopped when Billy Wright stepped in! Billy was great for me in everyway; I'd extended his career by a season and he repaid me handsomely."

Woking were the opposition in the quarter-final and they had watched Ashington and were afraid of striker Les Mutrie. They put two men on him so Jack took him out of the firing line and played him in midfield — which created a tactical edge — and they won 1-0. In the semi-final they met Bishops Stortford at Roker Park in a game which ended 0-0. Billy Wright and Brian Pringle could have scored but the England Amateur International goalkeeper Terry Moore made two fabulous saves. In the replay at Griffin Park, Brentford, the opposition, singled out goalkeeper Eddie Nesbitt for special treatment and he couldn't play in the second half:

"Tommy Dixon went in goal and we lost 2-0. I was bitterly disappointed; it would have been easier to accept if we had lost with our full team on the park. Billy Wright was devastated. He wouldn't let the hotel manager close the bar at midnight; he just took over as barman himself. I was a proud man, though, because my right-hand man Syd Bell and I had moulded a very good side and it was a great season."

Aside from his coaching skills Jack was becoming increasingly interested in the motivational aspect of the game, and chants, songs and whistle-blowing were playing an increasing part in his pre-match preparations:

"After the semi-final we played North Shields in the Senior Cup. We drew the first game 2-2 even though George Courtney the referee played nine minutes over. I threatened to report him. In the replay at their place Billy Scott was sent off after 15 minutes but we still beat them 2-0. Ray Wilkie was their manager and he said he thought there was a herd of elephants in our dressing-room we, made so much racket. One of my stars was Les Mutrie. I used to pick him up for training outside Burradon club at 6:30 but sometimes I would turn up a six o'clock and catch him having a swift half, then I would work him until he threw up. He never learned but he was a great player."

Jack was next persuaded to take over at North Shields, but it proved a difficult task. He worked extremely hard, and as well as persuading centre-half Joe Graham to stay he brought in goalkeeper Colin Revell and signed Davie Brown, Gerry Coyne and Vic Hillier. However his relationship with the chairman Len Murphy was not a smooth one:

"I reached the stage where I told him I would take them to the top of the league then tell him to stick his team; I got them to the top then put my notice in."

There was a lull in activities for Jack for a short while, then Jimmy Turney asked him to return again to Blyth Spartans. The rest, as the saying goes, is history, and what a fabulous story it is. It was built on a mutual respect between Jack and Jimmy Turney, two strong characters who both wanted to be in control:

"I had a lot of respect for Jimmy. He knew footballers but he wanted to run everything as chairman so we fell out, but we both had ambition. I was officially the coach at Blyth and I got the players and the manager managed the team. Geordie Watson was the Secretary and his signature was on the registration forms and he also scouted for players. George Watson was an exceptional secretary. Brian Slane was the Manager and we worked together; I was happy with that."

The first task was to improve the team's fitness levels and Jack was a hard taskmaster, but his methods paid off, and whenever Blyth played against professional sides they more than held their own in fitness terms. Team-building saw Terry Johnson, just released by Brentford, join the club. Tommy Dixon was already there; Dave Clarke, who played 14 semi-professional games for England came as goalkeeper and Ron Guthrie joined, as did Steve and Rob Carney from North Shields. Steve Jones was signed from Sunday football because of his electric pace; Ian Mutrie was recruited and left-back Alan Walker was signed from Berwick Rangers.

It was the 1977-78 season and Blyth Spartans were about to embark on the FA Cup run which was to immortalise Jackie Marks and his team. The fairy tale began at Shildon where the training, the hard work and the motivation started to pay off with a 4-1 win. Consett, Crook Town and Bishop Auckland were accounted for in the preliminary rounds and Blyth had reached their first milestone; the first round proper and a home tie against Burscough:

"I watched them at Morecambe and they were a tough side, I certainly didn't fancy going to their place so I was relieved to beat them 1-0 at Croft Park."

The second round brought Arthur Cox's Chesterfield to the North East and another notable scalp was claimed in a 2-0 victory, which left Cox distraught. Blyth's unswerving philosophy of attacking football held sway and they were through to the third round and another home tie against Enfield. At this point the side was further strengthened by the acquisition of Keith Houghton and Alan Shoulder, and by one of those strange coincidences which abound in football the Enfield manager was Ted Hardy, who had been in charge of Bishops Stortford when they denied Jack a place in the Amateur Cup final with Ashington:

"We beat them 1-0 and Alan Shoulder scored. He stood five feet four and jumped ten feet high; he was the hardest little man I've met in my life. We were listening to the fourth-round draw on the radio and we thought we'd been drawn away to Spurs, so the players were looking forward to a night out in London, but we had misheard and in fact we were away to Stoke City."

With the help of Tyne Tees Television, who made available video footage of Stoke in action, Blyth were well prepared, but the first game was called off an hour before kick-off because of flooding, and the pitch was still unfit for the re-arranged tie on the Monday night. The game eventually went ahead the following Saturday and Blyth came back from 2-1 down to beat a star-studded Stoke side 3-2. Garth Crooks, Howard Kendall, Viv Busby, Alex Lindsay and Roger Jones were all in the Potters line-up and to be fair the Stoke crowd gave Blyth a wonderful ovation not only at full time but also when they boarded the team bus for the journey home:

"When we came out to get on the coach there were 5000 fans waiting. I thought they were going to set about us but they gave us a standing ovation to send us on our way. We got home at four o'clock in the morning and I was at work by seven."

Jack's motivational skills had again played a major role in Blyth's preparation, not the least factor being a secret ingredient they called 'speedoil'.

"I carried a bottle of whisky and I made everybody have a small nip before they went out. We called it speedoil and when people heard about it I got bottles of whisky from all over; some people even gave me gallon bottles."

The night Blyth beat Stoke City, Wrexham defeated Newcastle United; Blyth were then drawn away to Wrexham in the fifth round — what an irony:

"When I heard the draw I thought 'Let's gan and beat them — I honestly thought we were going to Wembley. We travelled to Wrexham on the Friday night and it was so frosty we trained on the hotel car park; Barry Davies the BBC commentator joined in the five-a-side. As usual we sang on the bus on the way to the ground led by Rob Carney and Dave Clarke. Then we sang in the dressing-room and it went around the world on 'Match of the Day'. Then it was a nip of speedoil and out we went."

The game was played in atrocious frosty conditions which at least justified the car park training session, and Blyth led 1-0 through a Terry Johnson goal and were coping well, until one of the Wrexham players clattered into Steve Carney and the referee sent both players off. It seemed a very harsh decision as Carney was the victim of the challenge and showed no retaliation. To compound Blyth's misfortune the home side was awarded a corner kick in the dying minutes of the game which the referee ordered to be taken FOUR times because the corner flag kept falling down. Dave Clarke caught the first three attempts but Wrexham scored their equaliser from the fourth. Jack was disappointed to concede the late goal but proud and happy to have earned the draw which brought the Welshmen back to the North-East. He was interviewed in depth by Barry Davies after the game, the first non-league manager to be afforded the accolade, and when the team called at a pub in Chester on the journey home the interview was going out on TV. The landlady recognised Jack and they had a lock-in until two o'clock in the morning!

It was an emotional time, as Blyth became the first non-league team to feature in the draw for the sixth round of the FA Cup. Their preferred option was to stage the replay at Croft Park but the police vetoed the idea and St James' Park became the designated venue:

"There were 44,000 in the ground and another 10,000 locked out, so it was probably for the best. We left from Blyth and when we reached the outskirts of Newcastle the traffic was

Commiserations after the defeat by Wrexham

End of season in the clubhouse at Blyth

gridlocked. It bucketed down with rain — which meant it was a very difficult decision to leave out Eddie Alder, who was carrying an injury, and play Dave Varty. As it happened Varty had a very good game."

Wrexham scored early on through a dubious Dixie McNeil penalty and the same player added a second after 20 minutes. Blyth dominated the game from then on and, with Wrexham hanging

on, Terry Johnson scored a goal with eight minutes remaining. The players gave everything and the geordie crowd was magnificent but the second goal wouldn't come and the fairy tale was over:

"I was gutted, but proud that a bunch of local lads had given people something to enjoy. One bloke I know told me the two most memorable events in his life were his wedding day and seeing Blyth play Wrexham. People know me and know Blyth Spartans everywhere because of what happened. After the game we went back to the Blyth clubhouse and had a good drink, and we went to work as usual the next day."

Steve and Rob Carney received no wages for that memorable match against Wrexham. They had turned up for training the previous Sunday still drunk from Steve's bachelor party the previous night, and even appeals from the Wrexham players failed to persuade Jack to change the rules: besides, there was still a season to finish. Blyth won the Northumberland Senior Cup and the League Cup but not the championship.

Jackie Marks stayed with Blyth Spartans for ten more years, during which time they won the league championship six times, and he was always seeking to improve his already talented squad of players:

"When I signed Les Mutrie from Gateshead Jimmy Turney saw him once and wanted to call an emergency board meeting. He claimed Les was the worst player ever to sign for Blyth, yet 18 months later he sold him to Hull City for £30,000!"

The roll-call of quality signings over the years is impressive: David Craig, Ray Blackhall and Peter Cartwright, all formerly first-team players at Newcastle United, Dave Mitchinson, Stuart Grierson, and England non-league internationals Paul Walker and Peter Robinson, plus Bobby Scaife, Geoff Hart, Steve Baxter, Dave Buchanan etc. etc.

Every performance has its final curtain, and when Jimmy Turney retired in 1989 Jack felt his work was done. He had short spells in which he helped turn round clubs such as Gretna and Whitley Bay, and now he can be seen around the grounds of the North-East, often in the company of Paddy Lowery as well as scouts such as Glen Craggs of Middlesbrough and Jimmy Tinning of Newcastle United and the legendary Jack Hixon.

He is welcome everywhere he goes because people know that he has contributed so much of his knowledge, his experience, his motivational skill, his forthrightness and his heart to the game. Jackie Marks is guaranteed a place in the folklore not only of Blyth Spartans, with whom he helped to make an impossible dream come true, but of the North-East non-league football scene to which he has given so much.

JIMMY McCARTHY

The Sheriff of Benidorm

The 'Sheriff' relaxes at home in Benton

These days retired bricklayer Jimmy McCarthy has only a passing interest in the game of football. He spends most of his time in the company of his grandchildren, and two or three times a year, as he has for the last 25 years, he goes on holiday to the Spanish resort of Benidorm:

"I'm there so much they should give me a sheriff's badge."

But it wasn't always a life where family pleasures and leisurely holidays held sway. For many years football was Jimmy's consuming passion, and his involvement in the game in the Benton area of Newcastle in particular has won him countless friends and left him with a host of memories.

Jimmy's footballing story began during World War Two when he was playing for St Lawrence's School in Walker:

"Things were in short supply and they turned our pitch over to grow taties."

Like many schoolboys and school-leavers of the time his only opportunity to play football was by way of the boys' clubs which grew up in working-class suburban localities, usually attached to the local school. Jimmy played for St Lawrence's Boys Club in the Walker area of Newcastle, representing them successfully at under-16 and under-18 levels. In 1946 his family moved from the riverside to the Benton area of the city, which was to grow into a huge local authority housing development but which was then virtually a wilderness with just the first few houses in place:

"Benton was just fields and we used the one at Four Lane Ends to play football. There seemed to be more boys than girls and we played all night and all day on that pitch. We found some goal-posts from somewhere then the local council came and helped us with the pitch itself. It was such a wilderness they had to put four horses on it first to get the grass down, then they sent some men to cut and mark it."

Jimmy, who was 17 at the time, contacted his old mates at St Lawrence's and they arranged the first official match played on the Four Lane Ends pitch between St Lawrence's Boys Club and his new team. They didn't even have a name, and when someone said they should put the result in the local paper they christened themselves Benton Juniors:

"They were building houses round about and we had no changing facilities; the women would come to their doors in Whitby Terrace and shout 'come in here and get changed, pet.' We had some good players as well: Billy Davison and Brian Mallen went to Everton, my brother Derek went to Berwick Rangers, who had a good team. Then there was the likes of Wilson Doyle and Jimmy Robson from Byker, Dave Winter and John Murray — good players."

When Jimmy's day job took him to Stanley in County Durham to work on revitalising wartime Bevin-Boys' huts, he and his workmates 'acquired' the basic materials with which to build a hut which became the changing rooms at Four Lane Ends:

"All the estate mucked in. A building was being demolished on the local golf course so we got hold of an Aga cooker, cups and saucers and pans. We installed hot water and the hut became a community centre as well as changing rooms. There would be dancing and bingo. I must say the council were brilliant with the help they gave us as well."

When the adjoining Fairways Estate started a team some of the players left to join it, but Benton Juniors was now established, thanks in no small measure to the efforts of Jimmy McCarthy. Having played his part Jimmy gave up the game for a while and in 1949 began to pursue in earnest his other interest and talent, foot running, with his pals Charlie Farrier and Barnie Greenwell:

"Foot running was very popular. Spence of Blyth was the top man and footballers from Newcastle United like Jackie Milburn, Tommy Walker, Geordie Stobbart and Frank Brennan

The 'Black Bull' at Benton

all ran. So did Ray Wood from Hebburn, who played in goal for Manchester United. If you won a handicap race you got £50 and a medal. There was a lot of betting with up to 70 bookies at a meeting."

All six runners in a heat started at even money in the betting and Jimmy would have members of his family placing bets on him so that he could make some money for himself by winning his heat. He was a successful runner and won a couple of handicaps in what was a fiercely competitive sport.

Meanwhile, in the middle fifties the hut at Four Lane Ends was still a thriving community point:

"You got a cup of tea and a slice of bread and

jam for a penny. We got hold of an old piano from the Black Bull pub and this kid had a drum kit so we put in a wooden floor and started holding dances. We were trying to raise the money to build a proper social club and the community spirit was wonderful."

In 1957 the aforementioned Black Bull pub decided to form a Sunday football team to rival the nearby Benton Social Club team run by Stan Ging, which was already playing in the North-East Sunday League. The team was started by Jimmy McCarthy and Tommy McGarrity, who were respectively just 24 and 21 years old. Tommy's speciality was to send handwritten postcards to each selected player on Thursday with the weekend's match details:

"He was one of the first people to use the expression 'yours in sport'. He was a lovely writer and nobody else could write anyway. The mothers loved to get those cards."

Supported by the pub manager John Caine the team was an instant success, striking up an intense rivalry with their neighbours at Benton Social Club. Stan Ging and Jimmy were involved in arguments about the respective merits of their teams every weekend:

"The first job I got when I started working for the council was to put a new fireplace in Ging's house, and his wife told me to hurry up and finish the job before he came in from work. I should have blocked up his chimney!"

With Stan getting his hands on the best of the Benton Juniors players when they were old enough for senior football, the Black Bull recruited from the Fairways Estate, and whilst the rivalry was considerable both teams were very good and successful ones. There were two divisions of the Sunday League and Stan's team won the championship of the second division one year and Jimmy's won it the following season. Jimmy's father, Jimmy McCarthy senior, was a key member of the Black Bull set-up, raising money by selling domino cards, providing tripe and Bovril for the players after matches, and organising the medical gear:

"We used to get crowds of up to 1,000 at Four Lane Ends and we never cancelled a match whatever the weather. It was a horrible pitch, mind; it had a slope and there was an oil slick on it. There was a path running from one side to the other and women would push their prams across. Once a game was held up because a woman with her four kids was arguing with her husband in the middle of the pitch."

Despite the shortcomings of the pitch, the Black Bull attracted top quality players; Eddie Bell, Dougie Dunn, Brian Mallen and Billy Davidson.

The famous sloping pitch at Four Lane Ends, complete with oil slick

Alan Saunders and Ken Redfearn both played and they argued about referees to such a degree that Gaskell Irons, the league secretary, gave Jimmy application forms for the pair of them to become referees. They filled in the forms and in the fullness of time they both became top-flight football league referees.

After their matches the team adjourned to the Black Bull pub, where they would receive a bonus from Jimmy of a free drink if they won three games in succession!

"End-of-season presentations were great; one year we got Frank Brennan to come and there was a jar on the bar counter with £250 in it for the spastics. Brennan took it round the room and collected another £150. He was great. We went to his shop to buy a new set of claret and blue strips and he said if we would blow up 12 footballs for his window display he would let us have them for £2 down and ten bob a week. Another time we went to Jimmy Husband's house in the close season and asked him to do the presentation. He brought his mate with him who drank five bottles of Brown Ale; it was Joe Royle, who was only 17 then."

By now the housing estate, at Longbenton, was the biggest in Europe, and there was no shortage of good footballers:

"We still couldn't compete with Benton Social Club because they had strippers on a Sunday morning and Ging captured the best players. I wanted to give local lads the chance to play Sunday football and we had some tough lads in the team: keeper Ronnie Blacklin played behind a back four which was the toughest in the north-east; Ralph Widdrington, Terry Greaves, Kenny Webster and Davie Thornton. Their motto was 'nobody passes' — they should have been playing for the Bronx. We played the Five Bridges from Gateshead once and all their players were paid. They had this flying winger so I told Terry Greaves to cling onto him until he got sent off! 'Macka' Wright was the sweeper; no pace but a great organiser. We had skilful midfield players in Billy 'Dipper' Dodds, 'little' Ally Beaton, and 'Midge' Stephenson. Two ball-winners in midfield, Dave Allman and Tony Fairlamb, our goal-scorers were Graham Law, Paul Dixon and Kevin Carr. We also had Billy Allman, Dave's younger brother who was tragically killed in a car crash when he was only 20."

This was a very young side but a competitive one, which was capable of giving any team a good game. Their players attracted the attention of local scouts from football league clubs and Temple Lisle of Newcastle, George Hall of Hull City and Jack Hixon, who was with Burnley at the time, were all frequent visitors to the Black Bull's games. All of Jimmy's side made progress in the game, either as professionals or top-class non-league players.

Travel arrangements for away fixtures literally varied between the sublime and the ridiculous; if finances permitted a double-decker bus was hired, and as well as the players and officials it would be packed with local youngsters who were taken along for the ride and to provide support. When money was tight and they couldn't afford to hire a coach they travelled in a removal van:

"It was pitch black inside. Sometimes it was empty and you rolled about on the floor; other times it would be full of settees. Once it had a piano in it and we had a sing-song on the way to the game."

One Sunday a packed double-decker bus made its way to the Fossway in Walker, where the team was scheduled to play Daisy Hill in a cup-tie. It was a foul day and only four players had turned

Jimmy (standing on the left) with one of the early 'Black Bull' teams

up, the rest expecting the game to be called off. Jimmy didn't want to forfeit the match so he dressed some of the youngsters on the upper deck in Black Bull strips, then went to speak to the Daisy Hill officials. Thinking he had a full side, Daisy Hill confessed to having only seven players and conceded the tie; the referee signed the match form and Jimmy returned to the bus, which sped off to Four Lane Ends — surely the only example of a team winning a cup-tie with only four players. On another awful day in the middle of winter the team was involved in a home game on the notorious Four Lane Ends pitch. There was a four-inch covering of snow on the pitch and it was snowing heavily. They were using an orange ball and the lines were obscured; appalling conditions:

"Davie Thornton was playing centre-half. He was 19 at the time and built like a gladiator. His house overlooked the pitch and just after we kicked off his mother opened the front door and shouted 'Davie, get yourself in here; you'll catch your death of cold.' He's never lived that down to this day."

When the referee failed to turn up for a crucial match against Gateshead Three Tuns, officials tossed a coin and the Three Tuns won the right to referee. The Black Bull were 4-0 down at half-time, having conceded two penalties. Jimmy demanded the whistle and took charge for the second half, whereupon his team won 5-4. When he blew the whistle for full-time the crowd ran across the pitch:

"I thought they were going to lynch me but it was opening time and they were running to the pub."

Jimmy's refereeing talents manifested themselves again in a game against a Westerhope side containing several students, which was played at Paddy Freemans park in a hurricane. Playing into the teeth of the gale the Black Bull were a goal down after 20 minutes so Jimmy blew for half-time. The second half lasted 55 minutes with the Black Bull playing with the wind, and they ran out 2-1 winners. Then there was the time when two new signings had promised they would play but Jimmy didn't want to drop any of his regular side, so he sent 13 players on the pitch and got away with it.

Playing Scotswood in a game they had to win to take the league title, the Black Bull lost 1-0 and

Jimmy felt the need of a drink to drown his sorrows. There was a beer strike at the time and the pub only had lager on draught, which Jimmy detested, so he resorted to ordering barley wine and pouring three bottles at a time into his pint glass, unaware of the drink's potency:

"We had a presentation that night in the Benton club and I was there but I can't remember going."

The team broke up after that; Jimmy's father died and Jimmy and Tommy McGarrity lost some of their enthusiasm. He stayed for a year because his son David was in the team, and Jimmy recognised that the young side needed an experienced player to give the side stability, so he recruited Bob Morton. Unfortunately the ploy proved unsuccessful as Bob was sent off in both of his first two matches. However, he became

Young guns at the 'Black Bull'

involved in the running of the side and he was joined by Steve Black, with Joe and Ned McLean lending a hand:

> "We came out one time and there was already a match taking place on our pitch involving the Punch Bowl pub. Blackie walked onto the pitch, picked up the ball and told them to piss off. It turned out they didn't even have a permit to play there and had just been using it when we were playing away."

Jimmy realised that the new management team was a very capable one and they were working with a promising young team which included Jimmy's son David as well as Frankie Law, Larry Moat, Dave Woodhouse and Colin and Peter Rowntree. He was taking an increasing interest in the running talent of his 13-year-old son Paul, who incidentally was to become a top-class sprinter and a Powderhall competitor, and he was content to fade into the background and concentrate on helping to raise funds for the team:

> "I got hold of some catering turkeys to raffle one Christmas time. They were huge but they had no legs and I had to do some fast talking to sell the tickets. Steve Black used to have man-of-the-match awards with stupid prizes and he would sing a song with a clue to the winner in the words; he was crazy."

End-of-season parties and trips were part of the Black Bull regime; goalkeeper Jimmy Fawcett and the elegant centre-back Denny Quinn came back from one trip to Blackpool and convinced everyone that they had wrecked the hotel, until a letter arrived from the proprietor complimenting them on their behaviour and saying they would be welcome to return any time.

Many people are in Jimmy McCarthy's debt. He gave a lot of youngsters the chance to play football in a good, well-run set-up.

He gave Steve Black his first opportunity in management; a role which gave him his focus and laid the foundations for his future career as a world-renowned fitness coach. Alan Saunders and Ken Redfearn owe their distinguished refereeing careers to Jimmy's early promptings:

> "I loved it. The hardest part was coping with the parents when their kids weren't in the team, because I knew them all. It was all of 45 years ago and I still get cards and phone calls; they keep in touch, they don't forget."

45 years may be a long time, but Jimmy McCarthy has a lot to look back on with pride and satisfaction as he sits on the beach in Benidorm and polishes his sheriff's badge. Happy days. He is, however, anxious to make clear that running a successful football team is not possible without a lot of willing helpers, and he is quick to acknowledge the contributions of Norman Richley and Allan Saint:

> "Allan had a young son then called Robert who couldn't speak when he was five but by the time he was six he was as noisy as me and the players. I used to call him 'Jimmy's git' because I was always telling him to get this and get that. Charlie Crowe, the old Newcastle United hero, was another great help; he was fabulous with the young players. Everybody played an important part, including June, my daughter-in-law, who made the half-time drinks and my wife, Myra, who washed the strips. I still see Tommy McGarrity and I have a drink with my old foe Stan Ging from time to time. We are toothless tigers these days but we have a lot of memories to be grateful for."

TONY MONKHOUSE

The White Rhino of Weardale

Tony (left) training with Bob Tookey at Evenwood Town

Tony Monkhouse comes from farming stock in Weardale and he still lives in Frostley, just three fields away from where he was born and raised. As a youngster he had a healthy aversion to life at Wolsingham Grammar school; indeed he hated it so much that his parents bought him out. He did, however, begin his football career there, combining Saturday morning school matches with afternoon appearances for Frostley in the Weardale and District League before moving to the top of Weardale to represent Wearhead for two seasons:

"They liked me for my pace. I was very quick off the mark for two or three yards, then I faded!"

After two seasons at Wearhead Tony came back down to Frostley before the opportunity to play at a higher level presented itself:

"I was milking the cows one day when my mother came through and told me I had 15 minutes to get to the ground at Frostley. I jumped off the milking stool, plodged through the river Wear and ran onto the pitch. Tommy Whitfield, who was a player and a scout for Evenwood, approached me after the match and asked if I would like to play for them. I was told to report on the Saturday but I didn't know where it was and my father had to take me."

Tony's father, who was himself an accomplished all-round sportsman, maintained a small mixed farm with sheep on the fell and Tony did a lot of shepherding there. He had a talent for the job and an excellent sheepdog called Tess which had been given to him, so he was hired by local farmers to shepherd for them. This produced two significant benefits; the activity ensured that he had a high level of fitness, and it brought him a decent income.

To mark his debut for Evenwood, Tony's mother decreed that he needed a new pair of football boots, so she took herself off to the co-op in Stanhope and paid 19 shillings and 11 pence for a pair which bore the signature of Stanley Matthews but which were not exactly state of the art:

"They had a bar across the top and those pronged leather studs you hammered in. They were real

old-fashioned and when I got to Evenwood and took them out of the bag in the dressing room everybody went quiet and stared at them. Billy Bell was the manager and he took them off me and threw them in the corner. He said I couldn't wear them and gave me a proper pair. Those boots lay in the corner of the dressing room for two seasons and more."

Tony made his debut for Evenwood Town that day at right-half in a Northern League fixture against Billingham, and for a 19-year-old whose previous experience consisted of playing on unmarked pitches with no nets in front of crowds of 50 or 60, it was a major step:

"I thought it was the big time and that I had done well to get there. We weren't a very good side and we finished third bottom but I was lucky enough to keep my place."

Another development in Tony Monkhouse's football education came at full time in that debut match when the secretary Gordon Coe gave him an envelope containing £3. Tony handed it back saying he didn't play for money, but the cash was returned to him on the next training night and economic good sense prevailed when Tony calculated that by the time he paid someone £1 to look after the stock on the farm on match days and took into account the cost of travelling to Evenwood twice a week for training as well as Saturdays, he was probably out of pocket. He mentioned this to the secretary when he became an established Evenwood player and his money was increased to £5 on condition that he told no-one. Considering that he was earning £3:15 a week as a farm labourer, he regarded it as a secret worth keeping.

Tony had a wholehearted approach to the game; Jackie Marks once claimed that Tony had

Tony (back row, second left) in Billy Bell's up-and-coming Evenwood side

established a record by breaking one Blyth player's leg in a cup tie and another in the replay (both with fair tackles). His father, who was an undemonstrative man, came to watch him play in a game against Crook Town:

"It was a game which cut up rough and there were some tough tackles, and when I asked him what he thought he said I terrified people and he wouldn't come to watch me again. He gave me a good dressing-down because of my committed style but that was the way I played."

That wage increase had the effect of convincing Tony that he could do a job for Evenwood; if they were willing to pay him that kind of money they must value his services, and as a young player who never shirked a tackle he soon became a firm crowd favourite. In those days he had black curly hair and the ruddy complexion of a man who earned his living outdoors, and he was a happy-go-lucky character with a sense of fun, but when he pulled a football shirt over his head he wanted to win, believing that there was nothing for people who finished second. It would be fair to say that he was a very competitive player!

Evenwood was a side struggling to score goals in those early days, but with Tony installed at right-half they had a good defensive record, and during the next three or four seasons they gradually began to develop into a team which was capable of winning the Northern League:

"Bob Tookey came as right-back. He couldn't head a ball or kick with his left foot but everything else he did was great. Mind you, he was dirty. I clashed with players, but he kicked them. He was the first overlapping full-back I saw. There was this lad called Jimmy Connor, a flying winger from Stanley, and Bob kicked him so often he reckoned after the game that it wasn't possible to get down the line without the ball."

Manager Billy Bell began to recruit players from further afield to supplement the local talent in the team. He brought in goalkeeper Phil McNulty from Consett, then Colin Hallimond came to play centre-half and form a legendary pairing with Tony Monkhouse:

"John Suddes and I had played well together for a while, but when John took a week off to get married Colin took his place and John never got back in the team. Then he got divorced; it just goes to show."

Tony's own wedding took place on a Saturday, so some nifty arrangements were needed to allow him to play that day. He arranged for the team bus to sound its horn outside the hotel where the wedding reception was being held, and when he heard it he announced that he was going to the toilet. He slipped out of the reception, boarded the bus, played in the match and went home. The best man and the bride's brother took his new wife home, and his actions produced considerable and predictable disapproval among his wife's brothers:

"There was hell on. Her family wasn't sport-minded and they never forgave me, but I said I needed the fiver and she forgave me when I handed over the money. It was a freezing cold day and the match report in the paper said 'only

Monkhouse coped, with his sleeves rolled up as usual'. What they didn't know was that I'd had three rum-and-blackcurrants at the wedding and they kept the cold out."

Tony's commitment to the game and to Evenwood's cause was total. He worked hard all day on the farm, allowing himself 20 minutes to get from there to the training ground, and during his time with Evenwood, which lasted from his being 19 until he was 41, he missed only four training sessions!

The Evenwood team was developing into a formidable one, particularly in defensive terms, and the rearguard jigsaw was completed when Tookey, Hallimond and Monkhouse were joined by left-back Eddie Ross, who was a footballing enigma. Bald-headed, short-sighted and bow-legged, he hardly represented the image of a fine-tuned athlete, but he was capable of playing anywhere and in dead-ball situations he was lethal. Billy Bell's training methods also made a major contribution to the development of the side:

"Billy Bell knew what he was doing and we worshipped him. He was years ahead of his time and he used to go to Leeds a lot to study Don Revie's methods, and he would try to get us to play that way."

By now Evenwood were an excellent side, and Billy Bell added a finishing touch by bringing Ray Young from Wallsend to play up-front:

"Ray represented the new generation. He had long hair and we had never seen long hair before. When he went in the shower he used shampoo and conditioner; we'd never seen anything like that before either."

Billy's team was now complete, and when they

came close to winning the league championship in 1969 Tony and his colleagues knew they were a good side. They trained hard through the next close season with Billy Bell putting in a tremendous amount of work:

"He had us working so hard on sit-ups and weights that by Saturday we couldn't cough! Then he got us going on shuttles and I was good at those. I trained at home as well. I would run two or three times round the two-acre field, stopping in each corner to do a different exercise, and I ran in off the fells three times a week. If the Olympic Games had been run in wellies I would have won a gold medal."

The hard work paid off and Evenwood won the Northern League championship in each of the next two seasons. Success brought support, and one car-load even followed them to London for an away game in the FA Amateur Cup, though having got to London the occupants of the car had no money for accommodation and the players had to sneak them into their hotel rooms for the night. Tony found London an intimidating place. Before the game there was a ten o'clock curfew and a limit of two halves of beer:

"This taxi came to take us out and I sat where the cases go because I had never been in a taxi before. I was frightened of London; it was too big."

Back in the more comfortable and familiar surroundings of Evenwood, Billy Bell continued to introduce new aspects into the team's training programme; there was a team-building session at the Outward Bound centre in Bellingham, and on another occasion when the pitch was flooded and the team couldn't train he sat the players at tables of three in the dressing room and dished out sets of Lego, instructing the groups to build something

Down on the farm — with those famous wellies

so that he could measure who were the leaders, who were the ideas men and who were the followers. It was a sound strategy, but Tony made sure the curtains were drawn so that no-one could see them playing children's games!

Evenwood Town's Northern League Championship-winning side

developed to the point where it included both teams and the match officials:

"They were great nights. Bert Walton had the place and he served these huge baskets of chips for a pound a time. All the lads got together and the jaws slackened."

It was during this successful period that Tony had an opportunity to join Darlington, but Billy Bell took simple pre-emptive action, telling Tony that he had been a young hillbilly when Billy signed him and turned him into a player and he was going nowhere!

The defence of their first Northern League title was a difficult challenge because opponents were now familiar with Evenwood's style of play. Billy's greatest tactical skill was in organising defences, and Evenwood's was simply the best, but he wasn't so comfortable with attacking options. However, Colin Hallimond and Tony Monkhouse assisted him in this regard by supplementing the efforts of the forwards with regular goals from set pieces. Tony still loved training, and he wasn't above the odd light-hearted moment:

"Brian Mundell and I were doing sit-ups and there was an aeroplane looping the loop overhead. Brian said he wouldn't like to be up there in the plane and I said I wouldn't like to be up there and not in it. Everybody started giggling and Billy went wild and threatened to sack me."

Tony Monkhouse possesses considerable leadership qualities but he wasn't captain of the

Match-day preparation was another crucial ingredient in Evenwood's success, and Billy Bell regularly brought the legendary self-taught physio and bone-manipulator Harold Burgess through from Newcastle to massage the players before kick-off:

"Harold would give me a massage and I was so tense before games that when he gave me his bottle of olive oil to hold I would take a swig to settle my stomach. I just wanted to get out and get going."

There was no clubhouse at Evenwood, so the important business of unwinding after a match took place at the Wheatside Hotel nearby. It began, as these things frequently do, with a handful of players going for a post-match drink and team, the thinking being that it took the manager, the captain and the other players to look after him! His ability was recognised, though, and he had the honour of twice being selected for FA representative sides, once playing against Steve Heighway in his pre-Liverpool and England days at Skelmersdale and being hugely impressed by his skill and pace:

"Charles Hughes was the manager of the FA X1 and it was a great moment when I pulled on the England shirt. He told me I had come a long way and I wasn't to kick people or I wouldn't be invited again. During the second game I misjudged the bounce of the ball and kicked this bloke on the head and I never got picked again."

Tony's greatest ambition was to play at Wembley, but the nearest he came to fulfilling his dream was an FA Amateur Cup semi-final against Hendon. After a draw at Evenwood they went south for the replay, but Billy Bell put them through an over-vigorous training session on the morning of the match and in the closing stages they were effected by cramp and lost the game. That was the biggest disappointment of Tony's career, though Bob Tookey and himself were later taken to Wembley by Evenwood to watch the FA Cup Final, both singing 'Abide with Me' with a tear in the eye as they were swept along by the emotion of the occasion.

Time was beginning to catch up with Tony's playing career; as he remarked to Alan Wegg in one game, he was just about finished. Wegg agreed after Tony had kicked him in the chest during a challenge, suggesting that in the previous season he would have kicked

him in the mouth. So at the age of 41, after 22 years of unswerving loyalty, Tony brought down the curtain on his distinguished and totally committed playing career. His style of play had earned him the nickname of the 'white rhino', and a lot of Northern League players rested easier in their beds when Tony hung up his boots. His loyalty to Evenwood had been as amazing as it was steadfast:

"I had the chance to sign for Blackpool but I had stock to look after. I signed for Darlington for two years but always turned them down when they wanted me to play. Ferryhill offered me two wagonloads of coal if I would sign and Tom Hutchinson promised me £80 in my hand to sign for Tow Law at a time when I had a wife and two kids and was short of cash. I could have done with the money; I was knocking on doors buying feather beds and selling holly and Christmas trees to make ends meet, but I stayed loyal to Evenwood."

Evenwood Town team — Tony (standing on the right) as Manager

After his playing days Tony became involved in coaching, and when Billy Bell left he and Bob Tookey took over as joint managers, but Bob had a major row with Gordon Coe and left. Tony wanted to bring in Ray Stelling as manager and do the coaching himself, but when Stelling came he took over the coaching and put Tony back in the team. The move backfired, however, costing Stelling his job, with Tony taking over once more. In truth, he was happier with the coaching side of the game, where he produced good responses from players and was able to use his man-management skills, but he had no time for the politics of management.

Tony spent almost three years in coaching and managing roles at Evenwood before joining Consett:

> "It hurt me to leave but I had signed these young kids from the Consett area and when Consett themselves came in for them they wouldn't go, so the only way I could help them was to go to Consett myself. I was successful there but the town was dead because the steelworks had closed. The money was good but politics took over and I didn't really enjoy it."

There followed a brief spell with his old manager Billy Bell at Spennymoor United, but Billy's desire to control every aspect of training and coaching made the relationship unworkable. However, Billy left shortly afterwards and Tony took over, thinking the time was right for him, and during a two-and-a-half year spell he had his share of success. Most notable was reaching the first round of the FA Cup before losing 3-2 to Tranmere Rovers. Tranmere had Frank Worthington as player/manager and George Mulhall as coach, and two such high-profile individuals generated a good deal of media interest in the tie.

It was a highlight, certainly, but the following season Tony was sacked when the money he raised by selling three players was used to build a stand, leaving him no resources for team building:

> "That stand got me the sack as I knew it would, and when they asked me to join them in the Unibond League I refused. I was a Northern League man and events since have convinced me that they made a mistake in changing leagues. I had gone through a divorce and married Carol and I was trying to build a business, so when they sacked me the relief was like having a boil burst on your backside. Once I got the money they owed me — which took a bit of doing — I was away. Now I'm a successful haulier and farmer; I've got a lovely home and family. They call me 'day and night' because of the hours I work but I've come a long way since the days of feather beds and Christmas trees."

IAN MUTRIE

Archie's' Pork Rangers and Peter Beardsley.

Ian (left) with his late friend, Tommy Hunter

Ian Mutrie has always been the joker in the pack, from his days as a nine-year-old playing two years ahead of his time for St. Vincent's Primary Schools Under-11s, through his youthful graduation acquiring the striker's armoury of pushing, holding and shielding during long hours of one-to-one sessions in the street with his brother Les. Always, though, behind the daft-lad image and the ungainly style there lay a pride in performance and a striker's goalscoring instincts which combined to earn the respect of opponents and sceptical supporters alike.

'Archie' grew from a little lad playing for the school into a rangy youngster playing for the John Boste Youth Club at 15, and matured into a powerful 6' 2" centre forward playing for the Newcastle Employees side on their magnificent Coach Lane pitch in Newcastle:

"We had this deaf-and-dumb lad on the left-wing who played for England's deaf-and-dumb side. Great player, but frustrating. He couldn't hear you shout 'leave it' and if he was offside he wouldn't hear the whistle and would run through and score. We were a decent side, though, and we got to two cup finals."

Ian and his pals were brought up on Newcastle's Fairways Estate at Benton, where there was a public field which attracted the local youngsters who wanted to kick a ball about:

"However many turned up we just divided them into two teams, It could be 12 or 14-a-side. I was just a daft lad and so were most of the others."

One of the others was Jimmy Bradford, better known now by his stage name Jimmy Nail:

"Jimmy used to turn up but his feet were too big and he wasn't the best of players."

From those kickabouts on the Fairways field a team emerged which was based in the nearby Newton Park Hotel and which began life in the Whitley Bay and District League playing on a Sunday afternoon:

"Jimmy Fawcett ran the team and it was a great side, but we were only interested in having a laugh. We were strong lads and 'workie tickets' but it wasn't that kind of league so I don't suppose we were very popular. Our secretary had a three-wheeler car with four seats and for

away games six or seven would pile in. The rest got the train and we raised our money by running domino cards with the passengers."

Ian and his close pal the late Tommy Hunter recruited a keen 15-year-old winger called Steve Black into their company, introducing him to the attractions of Newcastle city centre and encouraging him in the art of stupid behaviour to such effect that he quickly overtook them in the field of inspired lunacy. There was a serious element deep within young Steve Black, however, and in his maturity he became a fitness coach of international reputation who helped Newcastle Falcons to their inaugural Allied Dunbar Premiership rugby union championship, before becoming fitness coach to the Welsh national side.

The Newton Park team's home pitch at Coach Lane was magnificent, but spectators were at a premium. If only they had known what they were missing:

"Before the game we would line up at the junction of the touch-line and the half-way line. One of the team took the role of the Queen and the captain introduced him to the rest of the players. When you had shaken hands you went to the back of the line, and we worked our way right across the halfway line shaking hands."

On another occasion, playing on the day after their Christmas night out the team took the field wearing the party masks from the night before. On foggy days they would move the corner flags closer to the goal and on one particularly foggy day they were playing against very weak opposition, so they made an agreement among themselves that they would only score from headers. Even allowing for this restriction they were leading 4-0, so the two strikers, Mutrie and Ian Yeats, left the field under cover of the fog.

Goalkeeper Jimmy Fawcett couldn't understand why his clearances kept coming back to him as his two strikers looked on from the touch line:

"We still won 4-2. We finished second in the league but we were so talented we should have won it by miles. We just didn't take it seriously."

The very young Newton Park side retained Ian's services for two years before he moved at the age of 18 to play for Nelson Village. During those teenage years he was also a member of a legendary five-a-side team which played at Burradon on Monday nights:

"We had a fabulous team with people like Tommy Hunter and Podger Parker. Peter Beardsley was about 13 at the time and he came along every week. He wanted to play for us because we were the best and we signed him on but we had to pick his games when it wasn't going to be too physical because he was so small. We still got up to our daft antics. We called ourselves Archie's Pork Rangers and when we shook hands with the opposition we would present them each with a link of pork sausage."

After two successive title wins the organisers wanted them to change the name of the team so that 'Archie's Pork Rangers' didn't appear too frequently on the championship trophy, but in the end the league itself began to fall apart and interest waned.

Playing for Nelson Village as an 18-year-old Ian Mutrie regularly scored four or five goals in a game, thinking nothing of it:

Ian (second right) in typical goalscoring action

"We had a great team and the Nelson Village pitch was outstanding, but Brian, the bloke who ran the team, couldn't handle us. We would put two shirts on and he thought he hadn't brought enough so he went home to get some more. He paid us £1 a game and when we finished runners-up he was delighted. The league presentation was held at the Wheatsheaf pub and we got better medals than the champions because Brian got the League Secretary pissed and swapped them over."

Ian's next club was North Shields, managed by Jackie Marks, who persuaded Ian to sign by offering him better terms than those available at Nelson Village. North Shields were one of the region's top non-league sides, and Ian scored the goal which took them to the final of the Northumberland Senior Cup. Unfortunately he broke his big toe and had to be content with a place on the substitutes' bench for the final against Blyth Spartans at St James' Park. Undaunted, he came on as substitute with his side trailing 1-0 and scored the equaliser in the eighty-eighth minute. He was left out of the side for the replay which North Shields won 1-0:

"The trouble was I didn't realise I had stepped up a class and I went back to Nelson Village after a season. It was a big mistake. I should have been playing at Northern League level, but I was as daft as a brush and I thought it was only a game."

Realising the error of his ways, he returned to North Shields to play for two years in an excellent

The legendary Blyth Spartans FA Cup squad of 1978

Ian (second left) in the dug-out with Jackie Marks on his left

side including Alan Barker, Fergie Donaldson and Vic Hillier:

> "I was glad to be back and I was happy playing to my strengths. I worked my bollocks off for the team, I was brave and I could score goals."

The manager then was the former Newcastle player Geoff Allen, who was a fine appointment in Mutrie's view:

> "He just told me to do what I was good at, which was laying the ball off and going to the far post. I scored a boatload of goals. He had a great

attitude; if it was pissing down on training night he would organise a domino handicap in the clubhouse instead."

Ian moved on to join Jackie Marks and Brian Slane at Blyth Spartans, and although he was in and out of the team he was very much a part of the historic FA Cup run of 1978:

> "It was an incredible experience. I remember scoring the winner in the fourth qualifying round at Bishop Auckland. They had an equaliser disallowed when it was two feet over the line, so it might all have been different. I scored the

winner in the first round at Blyth as well, then we beat Arthur Cox's Chesterfield at home. In the third round we beat Enfield 1-0, then I was left out of the team at Stoke City. They had Viv Busby, Denis Smith, Howard Kendall and Garth Crooks in the team and we beat them 3-2. We drew 1-1 at Wrexham on a rock-hard pitch and went out on the town on the Saturday night. We didn't give a shite about the replay then. Jackie Marks organised a pool competition and asked us all to stay in but only two stayed. Keith Houghton got the rest of us into the local clubs with his police pass."

So it was back to Blyth for the replay. The game was scheduled for a Monday night at St James' Park, but when the players turned up for the Sunday morning training session most of them were feeling the after-effects of Rob Carney's bachelor party the night before. Rob Carney was a major contributor to the dressing-room atmosphere at Blyth, making up jingoistic words for popular songs which the players would sing with tremendous gusto before matches.

The players met at Croft Park before the replay, had a meal in Blyth and set off by coach for St James' Park, only to find the traffic gridlocked on the approach road to the stadium, where there was a full house of over 40,000 with another 10,000 locked out:

"I was sub for that game; there was only one sub allowed at that time. It was my biggest disappointment that I didn't get on. It was a fantastic night and we came within a whisker of a quarter-final tie at Arsenal. Jackie Marks, the coach, loved me because I would work until I dropped, but the hierarchy weren't keen on my style. They should have put me on when we were 2-0 down with 20 minutes to go — they might as well have had a goalkeeper on the bench."

There was some small consolation in a two-leg win over Wrexham in the Debenham's Cup, and in tangible terms the players each received a three-piece suite and an engraved watch, but the double disappointment of cup defeat at the hands of Wrexham and being denied the opportunity to influence the outcome proved too much for Ian. He scored a hat-trick in the Northern League Cup Final win over Willington, which helped to heal the pain, but the squad at Blyth began to break up and he went back to North Shields to play first for Bobby Elwell and then for Jim Pearson in an excellent side which finished runners-up in the Northern League.

After an unstable period in which North Shields had three managers in three months, Ian moved to Ashington:

"John Tudor came to North Shields and he said anyone who didn't want to play could leave. He didn't fancy my style so I went to play for Chick Charlton at Ashington. Six weeks later we beat North Shields 6-1 and I scored five. Tudor didn't last the season and I ended up with 47 goals"

Ashington had a good side containing players of the calibre of Jimmy Harmison, Artie Lumsden, John McGinlay and a very young Tony Lowery.

Chick Charlton's assistant manager was Cecil Irwin and they led the side on a tremendous run in the FA Trophy:

"They gave us tremendous encouragement. We were away to Nuneaton Borough who had the ex-Arsenal player John Sammells as player-manager. I had a blinder. It was pissing down and we won 2-1, and they wanted Dave Brown and I to sign for them, but nothing came of it so I stayed at Ashington for two years then went back to Blyth."

Ian lifts the cup ...

people, but we still went out and played in a committed way. You still had to produce the goods. I didn't play with pressure but when you're not playing well it's still there. You've got to perform. You've got to have pride behind the stupidity.

"Micky Dagless was the manager at Alnwick and he was a cautious lad and his team talks were *so* serious. He was droning on once so I took a little green plastic truncheon out of my bag and said 'if the centre-forward is a handful Keith Muckle can hit him with this'. Then I got a toy hand-grenade out and said, 'if that doesn't work he can hoy this at him'. It was just a way of diffusing the seriousness of the situation."

That return season at Croft Park saw Ian score 15 goals in the first 11 games before the Spartans played Walsall at home in the FA Cup first round. In the last minute of the first half his foot stuck in the mud and he twisted his knee so badly that he wrecked his medial ligament. The next day he went to Sunderland Infirmary, had his knee encased in plaster, and was out of the game for four months:

"I came back and played in the last ten games of the season as well as scoring against Bishop Auckland in the League Cup final."

After a short spell at Brandon with Peter Feenan, Ian went to Alnwick Town, where the Mutrie antics again took the pressure off in the dressing-room:

"I could dissolve the tension and relax

Time was catching up though, and after a successful spell of management with Dave Studley at West Moor Social Club in the

... more celebrations

'Daft as a brush'

cheapest price. They lasted for years. The first time I wore them was in the rain at Crook and they had no studs in them. Jackie Marks said if I fell down he would fine me but I didn't and I scored a hat-trick."

Ian's brother, Les Mutrie, was a highly talented player who turned professional at the relatively late age of 30 with Hull City:

"I never compared myself with Les because he had so much skill. He should have been a top-notch pro but he went to Blackpool when he was 15 and they turned him down. He had loads of approaches from other clubs but because of that rejection he declined all the offers. The only time I played alongside him was at Burradon on Sunday morning. His vision and skill were unbelievable; he was a big game player and he had everything. It's sad, but he's enjoyed his life in a different way."

There remains one mystery to be solved. How did Ian Mutrie become so universally known as 'Archie' that many people believe it to be his real name?

"My old friend Tommy Hunter, who I loved, was my best mate for 25 years and together we used to wind my dad up, and Tommy nicknamed him daft old Archie. I was just as daft and the name was handed down to me. Loads of people still thinks it's my real name. I must say I had some great times and some great laughs in my playing career and I thoroughly enjoyed it. I worked my bollocks off every time I played; well, you don't want to be remembered as an arsehole do you?"

North-East Sunday League, the colourful career of Ian 'Archie' Mutrie came to an end. He no longer had a use for the pair of orange-and-black boots Blyth Spartans had bought for him:

"They provided everybody with all-weather footwear. I got mine at Parrish's store. I always got my boots there because you could change the price tags and get the best boots for the

Archie will be remembered as an honest and thoroughly conscientious player who scored goals 'for fun' and along the way he taught Peter Beardsley a thing or two — about pork sausage.

VIN PEARSON

Pride of South Tyneside

Young Vin (centre) on trial at Grimsby Town

Vin Pearson is revered in the towns of Jarrow and Hebburn in South Tyneside's industrial heartland for the quality of the footballing skills he displayed in those parts throughout a long and distinguished career as a creative midfield player in the mould of the great Jim Baxter.

His career began in earnest in 1962 when Vin left school and signed for Reyrolles Juniors, where he soon attracted the attention of 'Cop' Johnson, who was a scout for Grimsby Town, and he was taken for trials to Blundell Park. During his month at Grimsby the Town manager Tim Ward left to take over the reins at Derby County, to be replaced by Tom Johnson, and young Vin's skills made a clear impression on the hierachy at the club. To the delight of Vin and his father, who was with him at Grimsby to provide the support he always gave to his talented son, the youngster played one Saturday morning for Grimsby Juniors against Sheffield United (a side which included Mick Jones, later to distinguish himself with Leeds), then in the afternoon watched Newcastle United win 1-0 at Blundell Park thanks to a Ken Leek goal.

Vin enjoyed his time at Grimsby playing for the juniors either as a left-half or an inside-left:

> "I was treated like a god. They took me down on the train and bought me a meal on the way, but to be honest I was an only child and I was spoilt so I was frightened to leave home even though my father was very supportive. I had left school and started to serve my time in the Mercantile dry dock at Jarrow as an apprentice fitter, so when Grimsby offered me an apprentice professional contract I turned them down."

Another opportunity presented itself nearer home when Vin's uncle Mick Burns, who had played in wartime matches for Newcastle United, wrote to the Magpies' manager Joe Harvey recommending the youngster for a trial:

> "The Newcastle Juniors played on Hunters Moor at the time and I went along but there were some very good players around at the time like Geoff Allen who was a fellow trialist of mine, and although I did OK nothing materialised in the end."

So Vin began playing for Jarrow St Mary's under the management of a South Shields player of the day called Frank Weir, before graduating to Reyrolles Juniors as a 17 and 18-year-old. The highlights of the Reyrolles seasons were the

Young Starlet!

clashes with another team of works apprentices, Leslies Juniors, who included among their number winger George Armstrong, who went on to have a distinguished career with Arsenal, and defender

Ronnie Tatum, who captained North Shields to triumph in the FA Amateur Cup.

"George Armstrong was an unbelievable player. He had such tremendous ability it was no surprise that he made the grade with Arsenal in the pro game."

As well as playing junior football for Reyrolles Vin began his long association with the Robin Hood team in the North-East Sunday League:

"It was a decent standard and we were a good team, then Johnny Gatens, who was a very good winger at the Robin Hood, took me to play on Saturdays for Spennymoor United, who had Colin Richardson playing left-back for them. I loved playing for the Robin Hood, though. We were well supported and I remember once we took a full bus to play the Bugle in Gateshead somewhere. The supporters paid half-a-crown for a seat on the bus. The medical box was on the roof rack and when we went round a corner it fell on somebody's head and split it open. When we opened the medical box it was empty so the bus had to go to the Queen Elizabeth hospital to get the bloke's head fixed."

It was evidence of the ability as well as the resilience of Vin Pearson that as an 18-year-old he was playing senior Sunday football in a high quality league for a very good side which had started at the bottom and worked its way up through the leagues to operate at the top level:

"They were fabulous days. Dickie Guard had started it off and we had a great time after the games when we got back to the Robin Hood. There would be cheese and biscuits laid on, and turns on the stage, and we would have six or seven bottles of Double Maxim every session. They were great people and the crowds were unbelievable."

Combining Saturday afternoon football with turning out for the Robin Hood on Sundays presented young Vin with no problems, even taking into account the excesses of his Saturday night social life:

"My mother, God bless her, used to make me a bacon sandwich every Sunday morning. I'd have it with a cup of tea, smoke three tabs, have a good spew, then go out and play a blinder!"

His stay at Spennymoor was a short one. The level was just a little demanding at that stage in his developing career so he moved back to the more comfortable surroundings of South Tyneside to play for South Shields Reserves under the management of the former Newcastle United and Northern Ireland international full-back Alf McMichael:

"McMichael gave me the biggest bollocking I have ever had. He ranted and raved and he asked me who I thought I was. He said I looked like I had never played the game before, and he did it in front of everybody. After that my confidence was no good and I didn't stay for long. I would have loved to have made it at South Shields; it was only five minutes from home, but I had to move on."

He went from South Shields to Stanley United, another Northern League club, where George Midgeley was the manager. He would meet up in Dunston with Frankie Rankin, Freddie Shotton and Bob Joycen to travel to Stanley, and Vin would boost his morale and confidence by drinking two bottles of Newcastle Brown Ale on the way to the ground. It proved to be a happy and successful period for him both on and off the pitch:

"I was a star at Stanley. They used to call me

The 'Robin Hood', Jarrow, Sunday Team

Jim Baxter. It was a long way but I didn't mind that. One day I left Jarrow in bright sunshine and when we got to Stanley it was so foggy you couldn't see a hand in front of your face and the game was off. After the matches we would go upstairs for pie and peas then down the pub for three or four pints to round off the day, Great times."

After two seasons at Stanley it was time to move on again, and Vin signed for Ashington, where he has particular memories of playing in a testimonial match for Jack Charlton in 1973:

"It was the day after Sunderland beat Arsenal in the semi-final of the FA Cup, and Ashington were playing a Jack Charlton Select X1 at Portland Park. Jack wasn't playing, just watching from the touchline. I left the house that day in a brown knee-length coat because it was hoying it down with snow. Jack asked if he could borrow my coat and it had 16 tabs in the pocket but when I got it back there were sixteen dumps in the pocket. Never mind, we all got an inscribed marble cigarette lighter and he was a lovely fella; great crack, great man."

Vin Pearson never regarded himself as a person who sought the spotlight at Ashington. He was working in the shipyards at the time, and his workmate Micky Robson gave him a lift to training but he had to get the bus home to Jarrow. Kenny Prior was the manager and Jackie Marks was his coach, with Jackie later taking over as manager:

"There were some great characters and good players at Ashington. Eddie Nesbitt was the goalkeeper but nearly every week he couldn't play because he was a glazier and he kept cutting himself. He should have bought a pair of welder's gloves. There were Les Mutrie and Billy Cawthra, and Malcolm Robson was our centre-forward — good players. I think we were on 30 shillings in 1970, which wasn't bad. At Stanley we were on the same but we got paid in threepenny bits."

Family circumstances brought an end to the happy era at Ashington. Vin's wife was expecting their first child, which necessitated him working overtime at night to earn extra money, so that he couldn't train. So he turned out closer to home for Hawthorn Leslies in the Washington District League:

"We had good players like Brian Errington who was a big centre-half. I played there five years and then I finished. As it happened my wife had Christopher, our first, on a Sunday so I dropped her off at the hospital then went to play for the Robin Hood."

Throughout the years of his Saturday career Vin was also playing for the Sunday team which was close to his heart, the Robin Hood. Vin Pearson is synonymous with the Robin Hood and with the top-quality football for which it justifiably renowned. They won every division of the North-East Sunday League except the Premier Division and in addition won every cup during his time as a player. Distinguished players such as Frank and Kenny Storey and the McCaffrey bothers Aidan and Bede were team-mates, and truth to tell his Sunday League years with the Robin Hood were the happiest and most fulfilling of Vin's career:

"In the end my knees had gone and what with working six 12-hour shifts in the Naval yard to bring the money in I had to call it a day. I have to say, incidentally, that my wife was always superbly supportive."

After hanging up his boots Vin had two years away from the game entirely before taking his first formative steps in management:

"I started on Saturdays as Joe Anthony's assistant at Jarrow St Mary's in the SavaCentre League, putting up the goalposts and nets and shovelling the shite off the pitch. I believe if you respect the man you are working for you'll work hard, and if you haven't got it you won't get it."

After a successful spell at Jarrow St Mary's he moved to Hebburn for six years of further success in the Wearside League and the Northern League. He attracted high quality players such as the former Newcastle United trio of Kevin Caizeley, David Hallam and Paul Tinmouth, and produced a well-supported team:

"I bought David Hallam from Newcastle Blue Star for £100 but never paid the money yet. One of our best performances was beating Whickham 1-0 in a season when they hadn't lost a game. It was at our place and the crowd clapped everybody off the field, but Billy Hodgson, their manager, wouldn't let his players go for a drink with ours after the game. Then we played Spennymoor in the quarter-final of

Vin relaxing on holiday

time as well, with my brother-in-law dying from cancer. They were my own people though and I thought the world of them. I lived just across the road from the ground; the pie-man used to drop the pies off at my house and I carried the tray on my head across to the ground."

Vin dropped out of the game for a while after his emotional departure from Hebburn, returning to help Reyrolles in the Northern Alliance, where he just missed out on promotion before going to work as Brian Hill's assistant at Jarrow in the Wearside League. He moved to Easington for three years as manager before taking on the manager's role at Eppleton in the second division of the Arnott Insurance Northern League. The 1999-2000 season wasn't the best; Eppleton didn't win a single league game and conceded 157 goals. Vin, though, remained cheerful:

"We'll be all right next season; I've just signed two bricklayers!"

Signing players can be a bizarre experience around Vin Pearson. During the 1999-2000 season he ran out of player-registration forms, so he contacted his friend Tom Derrick, the secretary of Hebburn:

"I met him in the back of church one Sunday morning to pick up the forms. He was praying with his wife and he stopped to pass them across. It's the only time I've been given a signing-on form in church. It might be a good omen."

Let's hope so, because Vin Pearson deserves to be successful. His talent as a player was phenomenal and his graceful, unflustered style brought pleasure to a lot of people, especially those he still calls his own people, the folks of Jarrow and Hebburn, where his playing skills guarantee him the status of a non-league legend.

the Durham Challenge Cup and drew 3-3 after extra time. People said it was the greatest game ever. We had a great run in the FA Vase as well but when we eventually went out after losing in extra time I was heartbroken and I resigned in tears. To be fair I had family problems at the

MALCOLM PEEL

Ronnie Simpson, Harry Gregg and a man in a long black coat.

Malcolm holding the trophy in his safe hands

Malcolm Peel decided to become a goalkeeper as a youngster when he saw Ronnie Simpson play for Newcastle United in the FA Cup Final. Simpson's agility and poise inspired him to the point of obsession and from that day he had no interest in playing in any other position on the field.

His first steps on the road to recognition came in junior football with Wallsend St. Columba's, where he was spotted and, along with full back Barry Clark, he was invited to join Whitley Bay. However, like Bay's legendary centre-forward Billy Wright, Malcolm found it difficult to settle at a Whitley Bay club which was run by 'collar-and-tie' men:

"You never felt part of the club no matter how

well you played. Billy and I left the shipyards and went straight to training: you could see the steam coming out of Billy's lace-holes, and I never felt comfortable among those collar-and-tie types. The only game I played we beat Heaton Stannington 4-1 and I was dropped. I do remember one game at Whitley when I was playing for the second team against New York in a cup tie. It was the coldest day of the year but we had to play. Four players went off with exposure."

Billy Wright stayed at Hillheads but Malcolm quickly moved on, his first port of call being Crawcrook Albion in the Northern Combination League, where he was spotted by Bishop Auckland:

"They sent me a telegram telling me to report for a game. I got £3 and picked up a severe cut on the leg, and they provided a taxi to take me each way to Bishop Auckland. That was the first time I ever saw money in football. Bishops were a massive club and the likes of Harry Sharratt and Seamus O'Connell were there. I would have loved to have gone there but I was only a youngster of 19 and after just two games I went to North Shields."

His career was still in its infancy and his spell at North Shields was a brief one, hinging as it did on an incident involving Malcolm and the North Shields player-manager Frank Brennan:

"We were playing at Consett and their keeper kicked a long clearance into our penalty area. It bounced over Brennan and I shouted to him to pass it back, but their centre-forward, Glendenning, ran round him and scored. When I asked Brennan why he hadn't passed it back he told me I should have cleared it. We had words and although the other players knew I was right Brennan said I would never play for North Shields again, so that was it."

Malcolm's unhappy departure from Appleby Park proved to be a blessing in disguise. It led to the first stable period in his career; three-and-a-half happy and successful years at Blyth Spartans. Jimmy Turney was the manager, and whilst Blyth weren't the top team in the area players wanted to play for them and they had a tremendous team spirit. Turney, who later became Blyth's chairman, looked after his players well, and backed by a fanatical crowd the team produced some excellent results, including a memorable FA Cup tie against Lawrie McMenemy's Bishop Auckland side which went to three replays before Blyth were beaten at Roker Park:

"The Blyth crowd were tremendous, but the Spennymoor lot were real fanatics. One time they set fire to my cap and gloves and another time they pissed in them. You knew you were under pressure and the mob were baying at you behind your goal, but I just used to blow them kisses. After one game one of the fanatics came up to me in the bar and called me a lunatic. I told him he was the lunatic: I got paid to play and he paid to watch. Then he said: 'Why not sign for us? You're the best in the league and that's why we barrack you!' Spennymoor were a quality side but we always seemed to get a good result there."

Malcolm Peel's pre-match preparations were the stuff of legend. His game started when he woke up on Saturday morning and the adrenalin started to flow. His preparation was meticulous and he was always personally immaculate; he was totally focused on the task in hand and would convince himself that no one would score against him, that he was the best goalkeeper in the league:

"I was full of confidence. I put everything into the game and at full-time I was mentally and physically exhausted. I was inspired by the fact that I couldn't let my team-mates down."

Malcolm in goal for Blyth Spartans

Still at Blyth, Malcolm came up against his old pal Billy Wright, who was by now a fearsome, physical centre-forward. Whitley Bay had a well-worked strategy which involved them giving the ball to Kenny Sloan on the wing at the earliest opportunity; he would lob the ball into the penalty area and Billy Wright would hurtle in and clatter the goalkeeper:

"I used to counter that by coming out with my leading leg up, but one night Billy got over the leg and knocked my teeth out. I was literally sitting on the pitch spitting teeth out, but after the game Billy and I went home together without any hard feelings. It was a winter's night and I had a mouth full of stumps: I was in agony. We both had great pride in our game and that was why I later went to play for him when he was managing Ashington."

Malcolm's time at Blyth saw him develop and mature as a goalkeeper, and the opportunity came to play at a higher level when George Hardwick, the manager of Gateshead, asked him to attend pre-season training at Redheugh Park. Gateshead played in the Northern Premier League, which represented a step up in class, and the intensive three nights a week training was very demanding, but Malcolm soon made his mark. Starting the season as third choice it took him just three weeks to establish himself as the club's number one goalkeeper, and from that time forward he never lost his place, though he was involved in the occasional bizarre incident:

"One night at Whitley Bay in the mud our centre-half, Peter Whinham, laid the ball back into my hands, falling back past me in the process. I put the ball down to clear it and Whinham, who was looking down at his muddy self, knocked me over. While I was on the ground their centre-forward put the ball in the net!"

On another occasion Gateshead were playing at Bangor in North Wales:

"I was still working in the yards but I regarded myself as a professional and I had a great game that day. However, I was nearly sent off at one stage. The referee awarded an unjust penalty against us and there was hell on in the penalty area. I stuck the ball up the back of my jumper but the linesman spotted it and I was close to a sending-off. Their fans started throwing bricks at us and later in the game the ball was played through for their striker, Billy Conde. I came out and took it on my chest, intending to go down on my knees to collect it. Billy spotted what I was doing and grabbed my balls before I could go down. I screamed at the ref. but he was Welsh as well and he just told me to get on with it."

Malcolm was voted the best goalkeeper in the league that season, ahead of the likes of the former Manchester United man David Gaskell who was with Wigan Athletic, and his performances caught the eye of another fine goalkeeper, Harry Gregg, who was managing Shrewsbury Town. Gregg was keen to sign Malcolm, but George Hardwick told Gregg, erroneously, that he was a professional and would cost a fee. Malcolm was told he would receive a signing-on fee of £2500 but he had first to sign a professional contract with Gateshead. His mentor was centre-half George Siddall, and on George's advice he at first refused to sign the form, confident that he would still receive his signing-on fee. However, realising the club

Enjoying life at Gateshead with manager George Hardwick

needed the money he signed professional on the Wednesday night, expecting to join Shrewsbury on the Friday. Friday came and went with no transfer and a week later he was told there was a technical problem. In the event, and much to Malcolm's disappointment, the transfer fell through. George Hardwick left Gateshead at the end of the season, prompting Malcolm to approach chairman Bob Tulip to declare his intention of reverting to amateur status, having been required to sign professional forms under what he regarded as false pretences. As it turned out, he played another season as a professional before returning to the amateur ranks.

During his time at Gateshead, Malcolm formed what was to become a deep and lasting friendship with Norman Parfitt, a midfield player from Shiremoor who had been released by Bob Stokoe at Bury and signed for the Redheugh Park club:

"Norman became my best friend. He was an assassin in football boots but he got away with it because he was totally professional. To be fair, he only got involved if somebody else started dishing it out. He just 'did' them and walked away."

In a game at Morecambe Norman was having a ding-dong tussle with one of the opposition players, and as they passed each other Norman uppercutted him and the player was stretchered off. When the return fixture took place at Redheugh Park the Morecambe player swore revenge but 20 minutes into the game he was carried off again. When the two teams then met in a cup-tie he told Norman he wouldn't do it again and swung a pre-emptive punch. Unfortunately he missed, Norman retaliated with a third knockout blow and was sent off!

During Malcolm's time at the club, Gateshead never enjoyed great cup success or good fortune. Typical of their bad luck was a tie against Ferryhill:

"Jeffrey Lourie, a solicitor, was our chairman and he had offered us a fortune to get to the first round proper, but the referee sent Norman Parfitt off and disallowed two perfectly good goals. We were never going to win and we went down 1-0. I loved it at Gateshead, though. I was the only player who had his name painted on the gates: I didn't tell them I had done it myself!"

There was, however, a three-week period when Malcolm's wages were not forthcoming, so he sat in the dressing-room 15 minutes before kick-off in his street clothes. Jimmy Rainer, the manager, asked him why he wasn't changing and Malcolm told him he wouldn't change until he was paid what was owed him. Rainer promised he would be paid after the match but that wasn't good enough for Malcolm:

"Eventually he ran to one of the turnstiles and came back with handfuls of silver from the gate money. 'There you are, you mercenary bugger', he said; then I got changed and played."

One of the more unusual characters at Gateshead at the time was a player called Wilson, who was an extremely fashion-conscious man with an individual style of dressing. He turned up for games in a long black coat, and having removed the coat he then took off his jacket, shirt and tie in one movement, and after the game he would put them on in the same way. He emigrated to Australia and the last time Malcolm saw him was as captain of the Australian national side in the 1974 World Cup.

Training at Redheugh Park

Malcolm Peel had the distinction of playing for Gateshead in their last-ever game at their old Redheugh Park ground and in their first match at the International Stadium:

"The last game was very emotional, knowing it was the last time anyone was ever going to play there. The history of the club was there and while it wasn't a significant game otherwise, the emotion of the occasion took over. There's something special about the atmosphere of some grounds and Redheugh Park was one of them. The atmosphere at the International Stadium was poor. The pitch was never intended for football and they are never going to be able to create a good atmosphere with that running track in the way."

Sensing that Gateshead was a club in decline, Malcolm left after just one season at the new ground to join Bobby Elwell at South Shields for what proved a short-lived stay; he was there just a month!

"Shields were a good side. There were big crowds at Simonside and a great atmosphere. I wanted to go, but the first night's training all we did was run. The next training night was the same; we never saw a ball. I tackled Elwell and said I was a goalkeeper and needed to work with a ball. I told him I would have joined Gateshead Harriers if I had wanted to run. Then my wages were short; they deducted 30 per cent for tax. Gateshead had always paid the tax. So I asked for a transfer after a week and I hadn't even touched a ball. They put me in the reserves on the Saturday, which was annoying after being regarded as the best keeper in the Northern Premier League. I hated it after being used to such a high standard. At Tuesday and Thursday training there was no ball again so I told Elwell it was no good to me and I wouldn't do it any more. He just said they paid me so I had to train.

I told him I would never play and within 30 days I was back at Gateshead."

One night the Newcastle Blue Star chairman Billy Dryden approached Malcolm in the car park after training. His team was in the Wearside League and he was looking for good players and asked for Malcolm's assistance. He was offered £150 to sign as well as a good match fee and an allowance in respect of signing players. He took Billy Graham, Artie Lumsden and Norman Parfitt along with the manager Milton Gardner to the Wheatsheaf Ground:

"We put together a really good side. They gave us bags, tracksuits and boots, which was unheard-of. We were well-looked after and we weren't beaten in our first 20 games. Our first defeat was at South Shields and afterwards one of our officials verbally abused the players. The manager told him not to talk to the players like that and he was told to f*** off. At the management meeting on the following Monday night Milton Gardner asked for and was refused an apology and he resigned. The new manager didn't like us. I had an injury and missed training on the Tuesday and Thursday. It was agreed that I should have a fitness test on the Saturday and I was fine. I popped into the Wheatsheaf pub for a bite of lunch and when I came back I wasn't in the team. I was raging. It was obvious I wasn't wanted, though I did get back in the team and we won the double. The manager soured it, though, and after a season I went to Ashington. Billy Dryden had been great but the politics at Blue Star were unbelievable."

So it was off to Portland Park to renew acquaintance with Billy Wright, who was now managing Ashington. Billy had an excellent record of taking young, inexperienced players from junior football and giving them the opportunity to develop, and Ashington was an

Malcolm in action for Blue Star

Malcolm became increasingly disillusioned with the standard of refereeing. He recalled an incident from fairly early in his career when he was playing for Blyth against North Shields in a derby match which was also a cup-tie. The game was played before a big crowd and at one stage there was a skirmish between Kenny Duffell of Shields and Blyth's Jackie Embleton. Shields had won a corner and as Malcolm went to collect the cross Duffell punched him in the back, causing him to drop the ball for Shields to score:

"I said to the ref; 'Did you see what he f****** did?' He just pointed to the touch-line and said: 'Off! Swearing!' My jumper was nine-feet long with players pulling me away from him. Another time I threw the ball out at Shildon; the ref. was running towards it and it hit him on the head. He went down as if he was dead and the linesman came on and sent me off."

When Malcolm ended his playing days he had a spell helping out Jimmy McFarlane at Annitsford in the Northern Amateur League. Jimmy had been an elegant and thoughtful player and was a great reader of the game, and together they achieved both league and cup success.

Malcolm remembered his Whitley Bay experience and would never allow a player to feel uncomfortable, but he lost his enthusiasm when he found that the young players he was trying to help didn't really want to learn, so that his attempts to put something back into the game were thwarted.

exceptionally homely club which made players welcome from the moment they walked through the door:

"I loved the people, loved the place. The last game I ever played I took my wife, Chris. She couldn't understand what they were saying; she thought she was in Bulgaria!"

Billy and Malcolm tried to encourage good habits among the young players, emphasising the need to work hard for success, and the importance of proper preparation:

"I prepared very carefully and I'm convinced that is why I had very few injuries. I was a big talker to my defence: I learned that at Gateshead from players who were professionals. I wanted to be the best so I listened and I took the good advice."

Malcolm still posseses a safe pair of hands

Nowadays he contents himself with providing four footballs each season to a needy team as a goodwill gesture. He is a season-ticket holder at Newcastle United and he still holds some trenchant views on referees:

"Today's game is fast and there is some wonderful skill, but the biggest stain is the standard of refereeing in the Premiership. The size of many of their egos is matched only by the crassness of their incompetence. Pat Partridge and George Courtney were great referees and man-managers but now it's so different."

Malcolm's final reflections centre on the hardest of all goalkeeping tasks: facing up to penalties:

"I was at Northwich playing for Gateshead and they got a penalty. This bloke behind the goal said to his son: 'Watch this; he always puts them in the bottom right-hand corner'. I took his advice, saved the kick and thanked him very much for his help!"

Malcolm Peel set a superb example in his preparation and his professionalism. He set himself the highest standards and he took his work very seriously, but he played the game with a smile on his face; even if it was a rather toothless grin, thanks to Billy Wright.

RICHARD PERCY

To Wembley — via Percy Main.

Richard shows off his Wembley medal

Richard Percy first caught the eye playing junior football for Tyne Boys Club on one of those pitches in a public park which women are inclined to push their prams across during matches. He played against the likes of Willington Boys Club,

a side run from a terraced house by Peter Kirkley with iron discipline, which provided Richard with his first experience of playing against high-quality opponents and convinced him that he had the ability to pursue his dream of becoming a professional player. Opportunity first presented itself in the form of a trial with Northampton Town, managed by former England star Ron Flowers and legendary Welsh manager Dave Bowen:

"I went with Dave Buckowski and Tommy Patterson. They had a trainer who was a former sergeant-major and when we got there he asked me if I had ever done any serious training. Well, I was 15 and I thought I was fit. I told him I trained every Thursday night with the boys club! He made us train every morning and afternoon; it really took its toll on my muscles and by Thursday I was really stiff and sore. When I started sprinting that morning I tore a thigh muscle; I just couldn't cope physically with the twice-a-day training so they said, 'don't call us, we'll call you', and it was a case of back to the boys club."

Richard continued to persevere and prosper at local level and his successes included an Under-18 Northumberland Junior Cup medal playing a year ahead of his time.

Once again opportunity presented itself when the Reading coach, Geordie Ray Henderson, took him to Elm Park:

"I scored against Fulham Reserves and went five or six times to Bisham Abbey for coaching. Eventually they asked me to go for three months so that they could carry out a thorough assessment and decide whether to offer me a contract. They promised that if they didn't they would fix me up with a top non-league club. It was a tempting prospect, so I applied to my employer, the Department of Social Security, for a transfer. Unfortunately the regulations said that you had to have three years service in to qualify for a move and I was only 17 so I had to turn the chance down. To be honest I never really had the extra pace to get away from players and

I knew I would spend my career in the Third Division, so I contented myself with the knowledge that I had my two chances."

It was then that Richard moved, albeit reluctantly, from Tyne Boys Club to North Shields Juniors in pursuit of better-quality football, and with his new team he was again a Northumberland Junior Cup winner. In style he unashamedly copied his idol, Denis Law, with the shirt outside the shorts and the cuffs held in the hands.

By now it was 1970 and Richard quickly caught the eye of the outgoing North Shields manager Frank Brennan, who gave him his senior debut:

"I played one game for Brennan when he picked me to play up-front against Crook Town. We had a team which included a lot of good players like Ron Tatum, Mickey Dagless, Richie Hall and Tommy Orrick. In the first few minutes I challenged their keeper as he came out to collect a cross and he kicked me in the chest with his leading foot. Then they had this full-back called Tony Butterfield who growled at me throughout the game and kept tackling with both feet. I thought, 'this is a bit different', and it was certainly quite a baptism."

After he had played eight or nine games for North Shields, the club brought in Bobby Elwell as manager and he introduced players of his own, so Richard moved up the coast to Ashington and played for a short spell for Jackie Marks before moving to Wallsend to play for Marine Park, where he had four very happy and successful years under Tony Cassidy. Cassidy had a fine pedigree as a player, which included an FA Amateur Cup winners medal, and he was a progressive manager who on one occasion had someone on the line monitoring Richard Percy's contribution to the game. After the final whistle he pointed out that despite his claims that he never made a mistake, Richard had misplaced five passes!

The Northern Alliance in which they played was a good and competitive league and the Marine Park set-up, with its top quality clubhouse and changing facilities, was an excellent place to play. Tony Cassidy, helped by the hardworking Secretary Jackie Heslop (the only member of the set-up who actually worked for North East Marine), generated a family atmosphere in his side which included players such as Mick and Billy Colwill and Mickey Barry, and they had both league and cup success:

"The games kicked off at two o'clock and at first we played the game, got changed and went straight home. The pubs closed at three o'clock so there was nowhere to go. Then somebody suggested that we should stay for a drink so we bought a crate of Brown Ale and had a bottle each. The following week we bought two crates and the week after it was three. That tided us over until the Wallsend Engineers club, which was a big after-match meeting place for non-league players, opened at five. Then we'd call in at the East End club for one on the way to Battle Hill club. We had to be there for six o'clock for the Football Pinks coming out and by then we'd had five or six pints on an empty stomach and you really did begin to believe you had played like Denis Law that afternoon. In the meantime, your wife would be waiting at home dressed up to go out and you got home pissed at seven o'clock and tried to have a shave without cutting your throat to go out for the Saturday night. I was once in the passenger seat of Jimmy Gourley's van on the way home and we passed this woman. Jimmy said 'look at the knockers on her' and I realised it was my wife on her way out without me!"

During this period Richard was also playing Sunday football for Coxlodge in the second division of the North East Sunday League.

They were an outstanding side comprising young players and real characters; the likes of Billy Cawthra, Stan Bishop, Billy Blair, Jimmy Henderson and Dixie Armstrong, and they won the major Sunday cup competitions, the Drybrough's Cup and the Frank Brennan Cup despite being a second division side:

"About seven of us were playing in the same teams on Saturday and Sunday. We were just 19 or 20 and once we played against Swalwell who had Colin Richardson, Frank Rankin and Eddie Hewitt playing for them. Cawthra went through early on and he fouled their goalkeeper, so Eddie Hewitt and Phil Clark doubled up on him and kicked him from arsehole to breakfast-time, but Billy stood up and took it. It was a case of intimidation of a young player by two experienced adults."

From Coxlodge Richard moved to Byker Legion to play for John Wilson and Andy Kinchley. Byker Legion were an excellent team, sweeping all before them and basing their success on a sound defence then releasing Billy Cawthra or Paul Dixon to score the goal, which almost invariably brought them a 1-0 victory:

"We played on the Fossway. There were no lights in the dressing-room and you couldn't see to put your socks on. Those socks were legendary; they were so tight that if you pushed a shin pad down the front your blood stopped circulating! Our big rivals were Swalwell — who had Billy Cruddas and Colin Richardson. It was like World War Three and the games attracted crowds of over a thousand. They needed a strong referee like Lenny Burns or Ken Redfearn. Once, we were beating them 1-0 and they equalised with a shot from the edge of the penalty area. There were about 15 players in the box and as Billy Cruddas made his way back he was poleaxed; out for the count. Nobody knew what had happened but I found out afterwards that when they scored he had said to Mick Colwill, 'that'll show you, you bastards', and Mick laid him out with a short-arm jab. Nobody saw a thing."

The Byker Legion team went on holiday together to the resort of Arenal in Spain and on the first night John Wilson, a typical Geordie let loose in Spain, sampled a glass of sangria which contained a large proportion of local spirits. Liking what he tasted, he consumed an entire flagon, with the consequence that he slept for 24 hours, losing a day of his life. The hotel had two swimming pools, one heated and one cold, and when John eventually emerged in his shorts with his towel over his shoulder the players shouted 'last one in the pool's a puff'. They raced towards the pool and stopped on the edge leaving John to jump into what he thought was the heated pool on his own. His shock when he hit the ice-cold water quickened his realisation that he had been mistaken!

"The following year we went to Benidorm and Peter Cartwright clipped a Spaniard when we were out on the town. Before we knew it there were 100 Spaniards looking for us so we barricaded ourselves into the hotel. It was getting pretty nasty and there were armed Spanish police as well as angry waiters in the hotel reception. Ian Playfair had been in bed all day sleeping off the previous night's drink and when he heard all the commotion he came down the main staircase absolutely naked and still drunk. 'What's going on like?' he asked, and that broke the ice and saved the day. It was a fantastic four days but I'll never forget the mayhem Peter Cartwright caused."

The highlight of Richard Percy's career manifested itself in unlikely circumstances. Tony Cassidy took the bulk of his Marine Park squad to South Shields when Bobby Elwell left and as well as earning money for playing, his side produced good results, but the chairman wasn't happy with the style of play and demanded a more flamboyant approach. Players from the happy band of Marine Park brothers were discarded and Richard became increasingly disenchanted and eventually he moved to Percy Main.

By now he had matured as a player in his middle twenties and had added steel to his natural skills, thus equipping himself to play in the influential central midfield role. He was enjoying his football again and playing well. At the time there was a young and emerging side in the league called Guisborough Town, who had been formed in 1970 and were making a considerable impact. Richard had played against them twice and he knew that as well as paying their players, which was unique in the Northern Alliance, they were clearly a cut above the rest of the teams in the league in other respects:

"They were really a Northern League side in terms of quality but I knew I had the ability to raise my game and I played particularly well against them. I played against Jackie Charlton's son, John, in central midfield and I was really up for it."

Having impressed in those two games, Richard was remembered when John Charlton decided to emigrate to Australia, and when he was contacted by the Guisborough manager Mick Hodgson and asked if he was interested in signing he was excited by the prospect, knowing as he did that they had already knocked the two best sides in the North-East, Newcastle Blue Star and Whickham, out of the FA Vase.

In the thick of the action at Guisborough

"I honestly believed they were capable of going to Wembley and it was a once-in-a-lifetime opportunity. Mick Hodgson offered me £15 plus £10 travelling expenses and I signed. Colin Revill at Percy Main had the cheek to ask for a transfer fee!"

Richard made his debut for Guisborough in the round of the last 16 of the FA Vase at Ashby in Lincolnshire, where he was the only Geordie in an otherwise home-grown team. He went into the game with Wembley in the back of his mind and when Ronnie Sills volleyed home the winning goal from his cross in extra time for a 1-0 victory it not only brought Wembley a step closer but it gained him instant acceptance among the Guisborough supporters.

The next round produced a home tie against Windsor and Eton; a match which turned on a bizarre incident when Guisborough were leading 1-0. Their goalkeeper punched the ball clear and a Windsor and Eton player lobbed it back over his head into the back of the net to equalise. The ball was on the centre spot waiting for the re-start when the Guisborough players noticed that the linesman still had his flag raised. They dragged the referee across, and after consulting his

Guisborough FA Vase Final Squad

linesman he disallowed the goal for offside. The gods were with Guisborough that day and they ran out 1-0 winners and booked their place in the semi-finals, where they met Hungerford over two legs, the first of which was away in Berkshire.

Hungerford were a side with a good reputation and they quickly set about justifying it with a classy display which saw them take immediate control of the game:

"I told myself to forget about Wembley after a quarter of an hour. They outplayed us and it was like that all through the game. They slaughtered us really, but we managed three shots on the break in the first half and amazingly Ronnie Sills scored a hat trick to put us 3-1 up at half time. They pounded us in the second half but their shots kept hitting the keeper. It could have been 15-3 but we beat them 3-1. I remember thinking in the bar afterwards that I was really going to Wembley. I remembered my uncle who used to watch me kicking a ball around when I was a kid. He always used to say 'see you at Wembley' and now I was going."

The week between the two legs of the semi-final seemed to Richard like an eternity, and he wasn't helped by the fact that his adrenalin levels were so high he was unable to sleep. Family members, friends and work colleagues were constantly offering him congratulations and assuming that he was already destined for Wembley and that the second leg was a formality, but doubts crept in when Hungerford took an early lead and began causing problems, particularly through a pacy forward called Nevada Phillips. However, despite twice going behind Guisborough drew 2-2 and qualified for the final on aggregate. Richard recalls becoming very emotional on the pitch 20 minutes before the final whistle:

"I started to fill up with tears because I knew I knew I was there, but I had to get a hold of myself and play out the rest of the game. There was a pitch invasion at the end and the whole experience was an incredible one. You can't buy that."

Guisborough were a young club but they were also a progressive one and they prepared for Wembley in style. Phil Laverick, a local businessman, produced an impressive souvenir brochure, and before the big day the players were escorted to the Burton tailoring factory on the outskirts of town and kitted out with blazers, badges, trousers and club ties. The club did them proud. There was media coverage too, with Richard very much in the limelight as the only Geordie in the team.

The football club's determination to make the most of their Wembley experience continued, and on the way to meeting Stamford in the final the players and their wives were accommodated overnight in a top-class hotel in Berkshire. They had been waved off from Guisborough by the local

Taking the field at Wembley

Richard (centre) in action at Wembley

schoolchildren and the entire town was behind them:

"There was a lot of excitement on the Friday night. I realised my dream had come true and I was determined to savour every minute. We had been given £100 each for winning the semi-final but there was no money for the final; the honour and the medal were enough. I was totally focused and determined not to be overawed even though the drive up Wembley Way towards the twin towers brought a lump to my throat. I sat in one of the bucket seats in the Wembley dressing-room determined to go out and perform, and I had a good game, but the luck which we had on our way to the final eluded us. Our manager pinpointed their left-back as their weak player and he was right. I beat him three times in the first half and put Ted Coleman clear. Ted was an excellent player but goalscoring wasn't his strength and the chances weren't taken.

"Poor lad. On the day the chances fell to the wrong player. Then in the second half they scored and it was my fault. I tried to control the ball in our penalty area instead of clearing it and Keith Alexander (later to manage Lincoln City) sent a bobbly shot in off the far post. They got a second from 25 yards 20 minutes from time and the referee should have blown up then because it was all over.

"I was so disappointed I couldn't get off the pitch quickly enough and I bitterly regret not staying on longer and milking the atmosphere. Then there was another disappointment. I had been sent some lovely good-luck telegrams from people like John Downie and the lads at West Allotment Celtic and I left them in the dressing-room. The cleaners had disposed of them when I went back down. That night the club had a dinner and the guests of honour were two Middlesbrough legends, Wilf Mannion and George Hardwick. It would have been so much nicer to have won, and when we got back the next day the whole town turned out. It was so emotional."

Richard spent another year at Guisborough, playing in the Midland League, their Northern League ambitions having been thwarted by the 'closed shop' attitude which prevailed at that time. Then it was up to Whickham for a season playing for Jimmy Henderson, but that turned out to be a bad move as Jimmy tried to reconstruct the side following the departure of most of Colin Richardson's FA Vase-winning team. So it was back to Percy Main and a season which saw the Northern Alliance side reach the last 16 of the Vase before losing to Brandon. A work transfer took him to Preston where he played for Lytham in the North-West Counties League before returning to Tyneside and his roots:

"I was born and bred in West Allotment and I had been the team mascot when I was a kid. I played a season for them and picked up a League Cup winner's medal. Then, with Mickey Cairns as my assistant I had a year as their manager and we won the Northern Alliance championship. I took them to the last 32 of the FA Vase in 1987 and we beat

Mickey Cairns (left) and Richard enjoying success at West Allotment

Fleetwood Town who had won it two years previously."

If motivation was needed it came in the form of a piece in the Blackpool Evening Gazette which said:

"Fleetwood have again been drawn away to a nondescript North-East team; a team of allotment dwellers. No doubt Town will be hoping to plant a few goals past them."

Needless to say, West Allotment were primed and ready and with Richard opting for two at the back and an extra man in midfield his side matched Fleetwood for 90 goalless minutes. Then, in extra time, goals from Paul Lemon and Paul Appleby gave Celtic a 2-0 win and Richard Percy enormous satisfaction. The next round took them to Garforth but by his own admission Richard paid too much attention to the opposition and a game was lost which should have been won.

The Percy Dynasty

Management was an enjoyable experience but those who know West Allotment know that it is a footballing institution and the people who run it are totally dedicated. Managing the club requires 100-per-cent commitment and carries heavy pressures, and after one successful season Richard gave it up.

Not that commitment is a word absent from the Percy vocabulary, On the contrary, he turned his talents to running and produced an extremely respectable 2 hours 48 seconds finish in the London Marathon. The tug of football remained and he re-united with his old comrade in arms Tony Cassidy to play over-40s football for Marden.

By now Richard Percy the family man was devoting his energies to his two daughters, Victoria and Deborah, encouraging them to realise what sport has to offer. His encouragement has certainly paid off; their chosen sport is netball and Victoria is a member of the England Under-21 Squad, while Deborah represents her country at Under-17 level.

Their commitment mirrors that which characterised their father's football career; their achievements may well surpass his as they make their impact on the international stage, but no matter how glittering their careers turn out to be they won't be able to make that unique journey embarked upon by their dad — to Wembley, via Percy Main.

COLIN RICHARDSON

Semi-finals are for managers; finals are for players.

'What you see is what you get!'

Colin Richardson followed his father, who had played for Leeds United and been a massive influence on his formative years, into the professional game after a successful schoolboy career in which he captained a Chester le Street Boys side which included Alan Suddick, Norman Hunter and Colin Clish. He was wanted by several clubs and eventually accepted terms from West Bromwich Albion after a successful trial while he was still at school — a trial which was in contravention of policy and resulted in his being banned from schools football for the latter half of his final season.

During his spell at the Hawthorns he rubbed shoulders with first-team players who included Bobby Robson, Don Howe, Ray Barlow and Ronnie Allen, playing a solitary game for the senior side against Sheffield Wednesday and becoming a regular in the reserves:

"I had some trouble in settling in the Black Country; I couldn't understand them and they couldn't understand me. On the playing side they taught me how to look after myself and how to go over the top properly! I could compete and I could kick and pass with two feet so I made good progress. The regime was strict; you could only drink on a Saturday night, but I was very well looked after by Wilf Dixon for two-and-a-half years, then Wilf left to go to Arsenal and I didn't get on with the new coach so I made the decision to leave. They tried to get me back but my mind was made up. My parents took it badly and West Brom kept my registration, which had five months to run. I couldn't play so I had a rest and trained hard."

Colin discovered at this time that as a consequence of an earlier training accident he was suffering from a detached retina, so he underwent surgery, and when he was fit and free from his professional registration he began playing for Ferryhill Athletic. After two weeks he was invited by Newcastle United for trials, but after a month in which he trained twice a week and played a couple of reserve matches, nothing tangible materialised so he returned to Ferryhill, where his football education continued:

"Jimmy Sherburn was the manager and we had a good, experienced side. It was physically tough in the Northern League but it was a good learning experience and I was earning £5 a week in the local factory and picking up £9 at Ferryhill so I was doing OK."

Ferryhill and Willington, where he played for six months, were staging posts on the way to the club he was to serve as a player for ten years, Spennymoor United, of which more later.

As well as his Saturday football with Spennymoor Colin played for Dunston Social Club on Sundays from 1966. He had no previous experience of the Sunday game, but when he married a Gateshead girl and moved to the town he signed first for Teams before Eddie Watts took him to Dunston, where he revelled in the family atmosphere:

"They were nearly all Northern League players: Freddie Shotton, Frankie Rankin, Frankie Pearith. I brought Billy Cruddas as an 18-year-old; and the older hands looked after him. We had epic battles with the Birds Nest and Byker Legion; they were for real and we had big crowds. Let's say it was competitive! They were great drinkers as well: Freddie Shotton used to come straight from the Club A'Gogo with his boots wrapped in newspaper. He had been up all night but he always took two tablets in a glass of water, shook his head and ran around for eighty minutes, then went down to the club for another drink. They loved their drink and the crack after games was great. We stayed where we played then went back to our own club for the last pint. It was new to me but they were my friends and Frankie Pearith and Freddie Shotton still are. We still have a drink together every Sunday morning."

Colin remembers giving Frankie Pearith a pair of boots which had plastic studs with metal centres; they had worn down to the stage where the studs were like metal lances, and after a game against the Black Bull Billy Wright's stockings were in shreds and his legs were bloody as a result of Frankie's attentions; anyone else but Billy would have gone to hospital!

The Sunday adventure came to an end for Colin when Dunston, who had never paid players, said they wanted to bring in someone to strengthen the team and they would have to pay him. There was a principle involved and Colin, who was never paid to play on Sundays, left and spent a thoroughly enjoyable season at Hillheads before spending some time helping Jimmy Henderson at Coxlodge, then fading out of the Sunday League.

His Saturday career continued to flourish and Spennymoor were enjoying cup as well as league success. They lost to Macclesfield in the FA Cup when victory would have drawn them against Chelsea, and the following week they defeated the holders Skelmersdale away in the FA Amateur Cup in what Colin describes as his hardest game. Spennymoor scored early then defended for 80 minutes:

"There were nearly 3000 there from Spennymoor and Skelmersdale threw everything at us. Their fans even threw bricks at the team bus after the game. They were the top amateur team in the country and we beat them at their place. We won the next round and drew with Prestwich Hayes at home in the quarter-finals. Our centre-half was injured in the replay and this was before substitutes; we lost 1-0, but we should have won the Amateur Cup that season."

After his long and successful association with Spennymoor, Colin had a brief spell with Whitby Town before returning to Ferryhill with his mind set on a role as player/manager. He had always had a desire to coach and manage and after three months at Ferryhill his opportunity came, and ironically he made what with hindsight he regards as a mistake by giving up the playing side at the age of 36 when he was still fit and had a lot of playing experience. However, he had a nice little team at Ferryhill and some good players such as Stuart Grierson, Eddie Wilson and Andy McClusky.

He was at Ferryhill for just a season and towards the end of the following season he was approached by Terry Wood and invited to take over at Whickham. The club was run by a committee of Terry Wood, Jackie Gilbert, John Farrey and Harry Hodgson, with Colin having sole responsibility for team affairs. He won the League Cup that season and in 1979 took Whickham to the semi-final of the FA Vase. He had fashioned a good side: George Cook, Dave Callaghan, Micky Cogan, Billy Cawthra, followed by Keith Turnbull and Micky Carroll:

"I was absolutely gutted when we lost the semi-final to Almondsbury Greenway. It was the biggest disappointment of my career. I went to drown my sorrows in the Towneley Arms at Rowlands Gill and I've never been in the place since."

Lessons were learned by all concerned, however, from that Vase semi-final defeat. Players were added to give the squad depth as well as quality; Derek Ward from Spennymoor, Keith Knox, Billy Reilly, Paul Allon, Keith Robertson. A key signing was Ian Diamond, who had missed out on an FA Vase final appearance with Newcastle Blue Star:

"I gave him a bit of steel and responsibility; he was the conductor of the orchestra. He was a good passer and more important a good chooser of a pass — he took care. Mind you, in the semi-final against Windsor and Eton Diamond

Leading Whickham out at Wembley – FA Vase Final

he had a nightmare; he didn't contribute and I gave him a real roasting. They had a huge centre-forward so I switched Keith Knox to look after him and fortunately for Keith he was getting deeper and deeper — he could have been in a submarine."

Truth to tell, Whickham could have gone out in the first round of the competition because they were two goals down at Ryhope Colliery Welfare, and it took Billy Cawthra to upset the centre-half twice, receive two punches and win two penalties to help Whickham scrape through 3-2 and begin the march to Wembley.

Colin's carefully-laid strategy for the final was thrown into disarray when Willenhall, the

Wolverhampton team they were playing, took a 2-0 lead after 18 minutes, but two pivotal moments changed the game. First, the Willenhall goalkeeper was injured in a collision and the Whickham physio convinced his opposite number that the player had concussion and needed hospital treatment; the player left the field and was replaced in goal by the centre-forward, who had been causing all sorts of problems to the Whickham defence. Then, just before half-time Whickham scored to put themselves back in the game:

"I gave them a real roasting at half-time. I talked about letting people down who had travelled 300 miles to see them and about being an embarrassment. It was a question of coming out and performing in the second half, and we did. After 90 minutes it was 2-2 and their players were lying on the pitch and taking drinks before extra time. I told my lads they were gone and we would beat them. That was when the bottle came in and we beat them with character and heart even though they were a more skilful side than us. Then the elation set in. The only disappointment was that it passed so quickly. I didn't realise how big the pitch is at Wembley and when managers ask me for advice about playing there I tell them you can't defend high up the pitch or squeeze teams effectively."

Colin, his number two Jimmy Henderson, who was an excellent foil for him, and the victorious team returned to an unbelievable reception from the town of Whickham, where the streets were lined with people decked out in the team's black-and-white colours and the ground was packed with supporters. It was the happiest day of his footballing life, and as he is proud to point out, the last time a team from the North-East won at Wembley.

Colin Richardson was now a big name and a top manager in non-league terms and he was fired by an ambition to achieve bigger things; sadly his ambition was not matched by the club and he moved on the become the manager of Newcastle Blue Star under the renowned chairmanship of Billy Dryden. Colin takes the view that if you could manage Blue Star at that time you could manage England, but essentially he developed a good relationship with Billy Dryden from the first:

"He was hard but fair and he only wanted good players. I owe a lot of the success I have had to Billy Dryden. He had the vision and the work rate you need to produce success; I don't see that in non-league up here now."

Colin took nine of his victorious Whickham team

'We won the cup!'

to the Wheatsheaf ground but it took a little while to reproduce the success of his days at the Glebe. He was constantly watching players and earmarking the best; his vision of what he wanted was clear and he knew the job. He improved the players he had and supplemented them with top-class talent; Brian Magee, Kevin Todd and John Reach were integral members of his side:

"Reach was a great player and a great character, and he and Bobby Scaife were an outstanding pair of midfield players. Reach made his debut against Blyth in the Northumberland Senior Cup against Paul Walker, who was a brilliant player. I told him that whatever Walker did or said he should just smile and ignore it and play his own game; he scored twice and we beat them 3-2. He was the kind of player who gave you that bit extra when you needed it."

Newcastle Blue Star under Colin Richardson was quickly becoming a force nationally as well as locally, reaching the semi-final of the FA Vase before going out to Forest Green — who had major financial backing and who proved to be a better side. No complaints, but a definite sense of injustice the following season when they went out of the competition at the quarter-final stage against Hucknall Town. The rub of the green which teams need to win cups deserted them, and Colin asserts that the Hucknall game was one of only two in his 22-year managerial career where he was cheated by a referee. No FA Vase winning repeat, then, at Blue Star but a nevertheless impressive record of 29 trophies in nine seasons:

"It was a proper football club and Dryden was magnificent. I had great help from Graham Defty who was my assistant most of the time, and I was pleased to be able to give Billy Cruddas his start in coaching."

Nine years is a long time at one club even when success is as sustained as Colin's at Blue Star, but nothing is forever and he knew it was time to move on when Billy Dryden granted North Shields permission to talk to him about their vacant manager's post. He moved to the Appleby Park club, which played in the North-East Counties League, and he made it his business to develop a side which played what he considered to be pure football. Quality forwards Steve Pyle, Gary Nicholson and Neil Howie were already at the club and some shrewd recruitment and

top-quality coaching saw Shields develop into a very good side. The level they were playing at allowed them to express themselves on the field, and Colin's expertise encouraged them to do it against the better sides. The quality and style of football which North Shields produced and the absence of the daily pressure-cooker environment of Blue Star made his time at Appleby Park among the most enjoyable and fulfilling of his career.

After two-and-a-half years the Shields bubble burst; financial problems forced them to sell their ground and they were compelled to re-form and begin again, having lost their existing league status. Colin became a director of the new club in name only and helped secure their admission to the Wearside League, but by now Bridlington had expressed strong interest in taking him on as their manager. He had played against them with North Shields and had sold them three players; Ged Parkinson, Graham Jones and Dave Woodcock. He was aware of their potential; they had been to Wembley 18 months before and although they didn't have a massive spectator base they were a big club. The man who took Colin there was Ken Richardson, a flamboyant millionaire who lived on the Isle of Man and was Bridlington's prime benefactor:

"I took over in September and took them to Wembley the same season. I had problems with the race relations people because I sacked five coloured players who were hopeless, but they got off my back when I signed another coloured lad who was a good player. I had to change things quickly so I brought in George Scott as my number two, signed John Woods from Northallerton and Bryan Robson's brother Justin. I laid it on the line for some of the players who were coasting and in six weeks I had turned the club around. We won 26 and drew one of our next 27 games and we beat Tiverton 1-0 in

Awards night at Bridlington FC

Jones, who scored 20 minutes into the final and ran with arms raised into the crowd behind the goal in celebration. Unfortunately all the spectators were on the paddock sides of the stadium and he was celebrating to an empty enclosure, and to make matters worse the goal was disallowed for offside. As Tiverton took the free kick Graham was still struggling to get back on the pitch.

The chairman was naturally delighted with Colin's achievement and the vindication of his appointment, and the club seemed set for great things, but once again problems manifested themselves. Two months into the next season there was no money; the players hadn't been paid for six weeks. It transpired that Ken Richardson had bought a controlling interest in Doncaster Rovers FC, and Bridlington found themselves left in the lurch. However, two weeks later Colin was contacted by Tyneside journalist John Gibson, a high-profile character who combined his work as Chief Sports Editor with the Newcastle Evening Chronicle with the chairmanship of Gateshead in the Conference:

> "It was another challenge so I started again. John Gibson was a magnificent chairman and we supported each other. I got him to be more 'hands on' by taking him to watch players with me, and we used to meet and talk in depth every Monday irrespective. John knows a lot of people and he has a friendly manner, and I used that plus what I knew and my own ability to build something at Gateshead."

Colin was comfortable working with a top side and pitting his wits against managers such as Peter Taylor at Dover and Sammy McIlroy at Macclesfield, and the side he built at the International Stadium made a solid impact both in the Conference and in the FA Trophy. He was a

the final of the Vase. Actually, I hadn't realised we were in the Vase: I thought we were in the FA Trophy, and when I found out I was ecstatic, because I knew we could win it. It was better the second time; much more relaxed. I took them down on the Friday and stayed in the same hotel Whickham had used. They were ready on the Saturday morning and there was no doubt in my mind that we were going to win. Some of the players had been there before and that was invaluable because it is a players' day. Someone once said semi-finals are for managers and finals are for players and I believe that."

It's everyone's dream to score at Wembley and those who achieve it sometimes lose their judgement in the process. So it was with Graham

Richardson gets the 'Boot'!

and I offered to leave I shouldn't have, but there were things going on behind my back so maybe it was the right decision."

An unhappy spell at Doncaster Rovers followed; a period which Colin won't dwell on except to describe it as a nightmare, then it was back to Spennymoor, the club he had played ten years for and for which he retained a great affection. However, halfway through his last season he was told to reduce the wage bill by half. He took the view that you can't do that with professional people who are earning a livelihood. His belief was that the club didn't need a manager with his experience and profile and he left:

"I didn't need the embarrassment or the threat to my credibility."

That was Colin Richardson's last management post; he recently scouted and prepared match reports for Torquay United and, surprisingly for such a committed and passionate manager, he was happy to be away from the pressures, keeping his hand in by helping with training at Hebburn. It would take a good job to tempt him back, and perhaps the phenomenal support of his second wife Jan, which he is quick to acknowledge, has earned her the right to more of his time. A new opportunity has presented itself, however, and he is now number two at Bishop Auckland, and relishing yet another challenge to his skills as a coach. The trademark curly perm may have gone but everything else remains of the man who has contributed so much to North-East non-league football. With Colin Richardson what you see is what you get, and his record of achievement proves that to be quite a bargain.

full-time employee at Gateshead and he managed the whole club. It was the pinnacle of his career and the epitome of what he had been striving for over the years. Good as he was, though, there were times when all his talent and experience weren't enough:

"You think you've seen everything, but we went to Chorley in the quarter-final of the Trophy. They could have played us on the moon and not beat us, yet we lost and after the game I was numb because I didn't know why. It was a big kick in the teeth, then we beat Macclesfield who were top of the league the next week; I can't explain it. Still, the Gateshead job was the love of my life and I enjoyed every minute of it. It wasn't about money — I bought one player in four years — and when results went against us

TOM SHIELDS

The Guinness Book of Records Man

Celebrating entry into the Guinness Book of Records

Tom Shields' claim to fame is prodigious. He managed the Lemington Comrades FC Sunday football team with such a massive degree of success that their unparalleled achievement of 66 successive victories and 83 matches without defeat earned a place in the Guinness Book of Records.

Born in Highfield, near Rowlands Gill in County Durham, Tom exchanged the clean country air for the industrial grime of Lemington on the banks of the River Tyne with its glassworks, the power station and the Anglo Great Lakes complex as a young man. A sheet-metalworker by trade, he completed his National Service with the Royal Engineers in REME, and there he met his lifelong friend Clive Thomas, the distinguished referee from Treorchy in South Wales (of whom more later).

Tom played football for Lemington Comrades at the age of 20, captaining the side for three years, but his real impact began when he became a member of a committee of four who were elected to run the team. Early indications were not encouraging, with dissent among the committee members over team selection, and after an uneasy six months Tom argued that team selection should be the responsibility of one man.

A meeting was arranged to discuss the situation but Tom was unable to attend because of work commitments; nevertheless the decision was taken to appoint him as Team Manager with sole selection responsibilities, and he took up his post in 1966, leaving the other committee members with important but secondary responsibilities for administration and fund-raising.

A natural winner fired by steely ambition, Tom Shields began from scratch the task of assembling a quality side. In the early days he was hampered by the irksome restriction that all players had to be members of Lemington Comrades Club, but the task was begun and a significant early innovation was twice-a-week training, an unheard-of concept among Sunday footballers at that time but one which he regarded as essential:

> "A good footballer who is fit is a brilliant player:
> a brilliant player who is not fit is a good player"

was his philosophy, so he recruited a local schoolteacher, Jimmy Nelson (later to work with Newcastle United's junior side), hired a school gymnasium, and the game was afoot. At the age of 35 Tom Shields was on his way.

The team entered the 'J' division of the North-East Sunday League; humble beginnings bearing in mind that the 'A' division was the premier league. The early team was,

> "...a mediocre side with too many laid-back players. They didn't have my burning ambition. It didn't hurt them like it hurt me when we lost and a lot of them weren't good enough. I wanted better quality so I called a meeting and made it plain that my aim was to win things. Changes took place rapidly and it caused some friction among the players. Those who were still in the side would come and ask me why their mates had been dropped, so I told them that their mates should come and ask me themselves. I don't work through mediators. I was single-minded. The players called me Don Revie and some of them said I was too much of a perfectionist. I admit I had strong views; if 50,000 people said I was wrong and I thought I was right I would take them on."

There was much turmoil in that first season. Transformation was rapid in the pursuit of success, but Tom Shields knew that if he was to fulfil his burning ambition of producing a very successful football team he had to seek the removal of that rule requiring players to be drawn from within the ranks of club members. It was a difficult trick to pull off but eventually he was told:

> "You can do it, Tom, but if anybody asks, they're club members."

That was the green light he needed and the quest for success now became all-consuming. Hours spent watching matches, including junior matches, produced the talent. The principle of taking the team back to the club after games to unwind established team spirit, morale and a sense of camaraderie, and Tom was always there helping the bonding process:

"We won the 'J' division and the ball was rolling. Players saw what was happening and wanted to join us, but most of them were playing for other teams so I had to approach club secretaries. I've lost count of the number of times I was told to f*** off, but I just went to the players' houses and after I talked to them they usually signed. Their package included a token for a free pint, but only if they won! The man of the match, chosen by me, got two tokens."

Life was no paradise for the emerging Lemington Comrades team. They had no changing facilities and changed in the club, then carried goal-posts and nets a quarter-of-a-mile up the hill to the Valley View field. Neither were there any showers, and the committee provided buckets of water so that the players could sponge themselves down after matches. This was clearly an unsatisfactory state of affairs, particularly as there were three teams in Lemington who were all in the same situation: the Comrades, the Labour Club and the Social Club. Needless to say it was Tom Shields who was responsible for resolving the problem. After a series of meetings with local councillors where he made the case along with officials from the other two clubs, Tom was asked to produce a set of plans for the new facilities which would be considered at a meeting where a final decision would be taken. Among those in attendance at the meeting was the local Member of Parliament, Doug Henderson MP, who spoke for 20 minutes. Representatives of the three clubs were then told they could speak for three minutes each. The others complied but Tom was outraged and when his turn came he was going to have his say:

"I've proposed this, I've drawn up the plans, and now you're going to listen, I told them, and I spoke for 26 minutes. When I finished the first person to shake my hand was Doug Henderson, and we got everything; changing rooms, showers, tea-making facilities, the lot."

So the basis for Tom Shields' phenomenal success was established: he had the team, he had the facilities, and he had a winner's instincts and determination, but even he couldn't have anticipated that three years down the line Ross McWhirter from the Guinness Book of Records would be knocking on his door, though he does recall:

"After the first season when we won 'J' division I felt sure we were going to go places because we were winning so convincingly every week; sometimes by 12 or 14-nil. I believed that something extraordinary could happen. We were so together. Whenever we attended functions, engagements or went on trips we always invited the whole team and they bonded very closely. Success was breeding success and if occasionally someone stepped out of line I was down on them like a ton of bricks."

The social members of Lemington Comrades were very supportive of their team, but there did develop one area of conflict which it required Tom Shields' skills to resolve. After every match the players returned to the club and as they had always won they were in boisterous spirits, which didn't go down well with the Sunday-lunchtime bingo-players who wanted good order and quiet for their games:

"The enthusiasm of the players did cause conflict. People used to hiss at us all the time. It sounded like there were snakes under the seats. So a meeting was called to try to resolve the situation and it coincided with plans to renovate

Lemington Comrades — Cup Winners

the club. I told the committee that what was needed was a bingo-free room. They needed some persuading but the team brought a lot of customers in and there were plenty who didn't want to play bingo. In the end they agreed and built a room which earned the nickname of 'The Quiet Lounge'. The atmosphere in the club at weekends was tremendous. The footballers brought their wives on Sunday nights and on Friday nights the dancing was the best in the North-East. Mind you, I was still selling tickets for the footballers while I was doing the Bradford Barn Dance!"

The ongoing success of the team was attracting growing attention and one night Tom received a telephone call from Ross McWhirter;

"I didn't know who he was; I thought he was the tatie man!"

Apparently the people at the Guinness Book of

Records were keeping tabs on the team's extraordinary success as they were in the process of achieving their 83-match unbeaten run, and Tom was briefed to call Ross McWhirter each week to keep him up-to-date:

"He was a great bloke. He came up himself to make the presentation. I must admit I was very disturbed when I learned that he had been shot."

When the record was broken in 1974 Tom organised a trip to Spain for the players and officials which cost £69 a head for the week:

"Some of them hadn't even been over Scotswood Bridge before and it turned out to be an amazing experience. All the players went. There was Barnie Jelley who looked like Gerd Muller and was a phenomenal goalscorer. He scored 364 goals for the club and missed 5000! I shared a room with Peter Varty and when he was in the shower he produced a pair of glasses with wipers on them. One of the players in the next room had a woman in with him and Varty and I stood on the veranda to watch their antics. It was just made of wooden slats and it gave way; I came crashing down and nearly broke my jaw. We had trouble with bingo again in Spain. The hotel was in Lloret de Mar and they were playing bingo in the lounge. One of the committee men asked if the lads could be quiet while the game was on but I said they were on holiday and if the hotel wanted to organise a game of bingo they should find another room. At the end of the week we were sitting on our cases in the airport at 6 o'clock in the morning waiting for our flight. One of the lads had bought a guitar so I picked it up and started singing 'Quando, Quando, Quando'. The lads were shouting, 'Shut your hole, Tom', but the old ladies round about said, 'Leave him alone, he's lovely'."

Sadly, the indulgences of Spain took their toll and

after the following Sunday's match it was Tom's painful task to call Ross McWhirter and inform him that the unbeaten run was over. Lemington lost, ironically, to Lemington Social Club. The defeat hurt Tom particularly as he had set his heart on achieving 100 matches undefeated, but the pressure had been mounting and teams had gone to extraordinary lengths to try to end Lemington's run. One team played an unregistered player and when this was discovered their record was expunged, which did Lemington no favours, as they had beaten the team in question twice and therefore forfeited four points, while the team immediately below them in second place had only played them once and thus lost two points. Seething at what he regarded as an injustice, Tom Shields appealed to the Football Association and a hearing took place at the Royal Turks Head Hotel in Newcastle. Tom's argument that it was unfair to deduct points from his team when they were blameless was upheld and the FA rapped the North-East Sunday League over the knuckles for their handling of the affair:

"The FA marked the occasion by giving me a book commemorating the history of football and a copy of the official rule book. They should have given that to the Sunday League officials."

The Guinness Book of Records presentation evening at the Comrades Club was an unforgettable occasion. A capacity audience, which included Stan Seymour in his capacity as Chairman of the Northumberland Football Association, as well as Lawrie McMenemy, Keith Burkinshaw and Clive Thomas, saw Ross McWhirter present the club with a commemorative shield. It was Tom Shields' pleasant task to introduce the guests and the players, and to give thanks to everyone for their support on a historic occasion which must have

Presentation night with guest Frank Clark (ex-Newcastle United) sitting third from the left

impacted particularly on those three or four players who had been in the squad throughout:

"You couldn't keep them all. There had to be changes. That was where I had to be strong, but it was necessary. Anyway, the lads who lost their places stayed loyal because of the wonderful camaraderie. Mind you, all that commitment took its toll on everybody. There were so many divorces the solicitor told me if there was one more I could have mine for nowt!"

That was the end of an era, but the friendship Tom Shields formed with Clive Thomas in their army days remains steadfast. It is based on mutual respect and similar approaches to life. Their meetings over the years have been regular, and whenever Tom arranged charity matches he could rely on Clive to perform the refereeing duties. Notable sums of money were raised for the victims of the Zeebrugge Ferry tragedy, the Hillsborough Disaster Fund and families of those who perished in the Gulf War. In fact, Tom and his team raised £6000 for Gulf war victims, and when he asked the lady administrator from the fund at the presentation ceremony what he should do with the money,

"She said that if I gave it to her she would give me a receipt and transfer the money into the general fund. I wasn't having that. I told her three lads from the North-East had been killed in the War and I wanted their families to benefit. She said she couldn't guarantee that so I said she wasn't getting the money. I got the three addresses from her and sent the money direct to the families. It was a stand that was greatly appreciated by the people at the club and by the families, who sent the most wonderful letters of thanks."

It should surprise no one that Clive Thomas was such a willing participant in those fund-raising matches. No one know knows him better than Tom Shields:

"Clive Thomas is amazing. In the army he was excused boots because of his feet, then in civvy street he spent his working hours running around in football boots. I'm his closest friend and we're totally honest with each other, so let me tell you about the biggest incident in Clive's refereeing career, the disallowed goal on the stroke of full-time in the 1974 World Cup match between Brazil and Sweden. Brazil were awarded a corner and if they had taken it straight away there wouldn't have been a problem, but they started messing about even though the 90 minutes were up. One player left it for another then he left it for a third, so it was well over time when the kick was eventually taken. Clive blew for the end of the game as the ball was in the air. He was at the far post as the ball fell to the feet of Zico at the near post; the Swedish defenders heard the whistle and stopped playing when they could have challenged for the ball. Zico went crazy but Clive knew he was right. At the reception after the game everyone spoke to him and no one said he was wrong, but when he went to his room to collect his bags he met Havelange, the FIFA president. He told Clive he had done well in the game but that Zico's goal should have stood. He went on to tell Clive that he would never referee another World Cup match, and he never did. He was very bitter that one man could make such a decision. He felt

Clive Thomas (left), Frankie Vaughan (centre) and Tom

that if there was a problem there should be a proper hearing."

Tom remembers the first occasion on which he met Mrs Thomas. It was at Wembley when Newcastle United played Manchester City in the final of the League Cup. Clive was fourth official that day, with the refereeing job going to Jack Taylor:

"I had a seat right beside the Royal Box and Clive came over to see me before the game. He introduced me to his wife Beryl who was sitting just behind me. I said to her what a pity it was that Jack Taylor was refereeing instead of Clive, little realising that the lady sitting next to Beryl was Jack Taylor's wife!"

Tom is no longer directly involved with Lemington Comrades FC but his enthusiasm for

Tom (left) receiving an award from Micky Burns

the game is undiminished. A fanatical Newcastle United season-ticket holder, he's not afraid to express his views, whether it's in the press, on radio or indeed on Sky TV where he made his views on ex-Newcastle manager Kenny Dalglish known in typically trenchant manner:

"I was on a phone-in and I told them that Kevin Keegan had taken us to second place in the Premiership in successive seasons. We were a whisker away from Manchester United. Then Kenny Dalglish took over. He'd spent £83 million of Jack Walker's money and left Blackburn with a bad side and he sold all of our star players. He even fought with David Ginola on the training pitch. On the programme Rodney Marsh said Dalglish should have been given more time. I said I would have given him time all right but it would have been in Durham Prison."

Tom believes today's players are over-protected at every level and that this has had a detrimental effect on their passion and determination:

"They're faster and fitter now but the will isn't there and money has devastated the game."

He has a point. After all, Tom Shields produced a team which carried its own goal-posts a quarter-of-a-mile up a hill to play and cleaned up in buckets of cold water afterwards, but with their talent and his steel they ended up in the Guinness Book of Records.

ALEX SMAILES

Shooting from the hip.

Alex holds the Worthington Cup

Alex Smailes wasn't a gifted footballer. He played at school and boys club level as a right-winger whose principal attribute was his ability to cross the ball, and he enjoyed playing alongside his friends John Gay, Dennis Wilson, Geoff McIntosh and others. Later, watching Whitley Bay St Edward's, who had quality players in Harry Milburn, David Chaffey, Derek Adcock and

West Allotment Celtic FC in the 1970's

Benny Williams and toughness in Derek Stoneham, Brian McNally and Dave Newstead, made him aware of his own limitations, and he began in his early twenties to make what has been a major contribution to the game as a manager, an administrator and a scout.

His earliest reflective imput into the game came with his interest in photography in his late teens, when he would visit local games and take photographs of the action, which he began to supplement with match reports for the local newspaper. This was the germ which later developed into the incredibly detailed and perceptive scouting reports he now produces for Liverpool Football Club. He also recognised a need to provide playing opportunities for young footballers who were coming to the end of their junior careers, and he helped form a Sunday team to provide a chance for them to bridge the gap to senior football. The team was initially known as Seatonville but through Alex's friendship with Jack Tait, the late chairman of Whitley Bay Football Club, the team moved from its pitch at Langley Park in Monkseaton to play at Whitley's Hillheads ground, changing its name to Seahorse, the emblem of Whitley Bay.

Alex began managing the side at the age of 22 and stayed for four successful years:

"Our main competition was always from teams in the North Shields area. It had been the same at boys' club level. The great thing about the Seahorse was the loyalty of the players. The Sunday League were red hot with their fines and one Sunday morning I was waiting at the St Peter's Road pitches; I was early as usual and eight of the players were late. I was doing my nut on the touch line but the players got changed on the top deck of the local bus and went straight onto the pitch to play."

To say that Alex Smailes calls a spade a spade is like saying Pavarotti sings a bit. He has always been forthright to the point where he engenders feelings of polarity. People love him or hate him, though it would be fair to say that those who know him best, and especially those players whose cause he has always championed with a passion, are more likely to fall into the former category. His loyalty to players was a major characteristic of his successful years with West Allotment Celtic, the club with which he made his reputation both as a manager and as an organiser and to which he devoted 21 years of his life:

"Ray Taylor knew me from the Seatonville days and he was playing for West Allotment so he recommended me to them. They were playing in the North-East Amateur League and John Jackson — the Fuhrer — was running the side. I began working with John in 1974 as joint manager and the first task I had was to tell some of the younger players that if they wanted regular football they should look elsewhere."

West Allotment in 1974 had the nucleus of an outstanding team; goalkeeper Ronnie Blacklin was a real character who allegedly asked for a bell inside the ball because his 'lamps were dodgy'; Derek Stoneman was a top-class defender, and Benny Williams a prolific goalscorer who averaged a goal a game in over 400 appearances, usually playing alongside Ray Taylor, plus Davie Newstead, David Chaffey and Harry Milburn:

"I was green, but I knew about the players in the team and I always put them first. One of the pluses was our pitch at Backworth Welfare; it was like going to your own Wembley every week, and being involved in the management of Allotment was a challenge and an honour."

The team was built on character and commitment — what Alex Smailes calls the old values — and he saw it as his function to build on those qualities and to improve the organisation of the club, a task which wasn't difficult because the committee as well as the players shared his ambition and determination to succeed:

"I was extremely volatile and I wanted to be a winner but it took me a couple of years as I imposed my personality on the team. Then we reached two cup finals. We lost the Northumberland Minor Cup but we won the Northumberland Amateur Cup in the last year of its competition."

Coach David Cope had been an essential part of the set-up because Alex couldn't coach; his forte was as a manager and to those ends he was prepared to be ruthless, which is why he ruffled a few feathers. His prime regard was still for his players, whether they were in the side or not, and one of his abiding principles was to talk to players who weren't selected and tell them why, away from the dressing room. He was constantly on the lookout for better players. He recruited Dave Allman, who brought along his younger brother Billy:

"Billy earned the nickname of Alf Tupper and he later died tragically in a road accident. I always preached good football and by now I had stamped my authority on the team. Players themselves brought players because of the kind of club we had created."

Alex's passion was all-consuming and his will to win was paramount. If you were to search for a word to describe the way his passion manifested itself in his behaviour on the touchline during games you would probably stop at 'lunatic.' He contested every decision and made himself unpopular with referees and opponents alike. He frequently found himself in hot water with authority but what was beyond dispute was his total commitment to West Allotment, and the players responded to his running of a very successful club as he built on the work done by John Jackson in bringing about a resurgence of the club's fortunes when they fell away from their high success of the 1950's.

He continued both to build and to innovate. Daz Ridley, a phenomenal goalscorer and amazing character, joined the club to add another playing dimension. Alex introduced after-match buffets which initially he paid for himself, as part of his continuing quest for higher standards:

"We introduced the buffets after training as well because players were coming straight from work and it was something they appreciated. They loved the crack and the atmosphere and they

stayed with us when they could have gone on to play at a higher level."

Another of Alex's innovations was end-of-season presentations in the mansion at Backworth welfare, with awards for the player and young player of the year. Small envelopes were distributed at these functions which ensured that players remained with the club until the end of the season! Alex began to use his expanding list of contacts in the game to bring the likes of Joe Harvey, Tommy Cavanagh and John Gibson to make the presentations. As with everything with which he was involved, professionalism was his watchword:

"Rob Hindmarsh was a 19-year-old player with Sunderland at the time and he played golf at Backworth, so I asked him to do some training for us. His professionalism rubbed off and even the older players respected him. Ray Kennedy took some sessions for us as well."

The quality of players remained high: Chris Kelly, a player with enormous talent who turned up to play in a trial at Newcastle United wearing pink socks, as well as Micky Richardson and Daz Ridley. There was an occasion when Richardson and Ridley had been fooling around during one of Rob Hindmarsh's training sessions and Rob sought Alex's advice, as a consequence of which Rob gave the pair of them a massive dressing-down and told them not to come again if they had the wrong attitude. He then made them do 50-press-ups each; the three of them became in Alex's words 'as thick as thieves' — testimony to his man-management skills.

The success continued and another significant 'off-the-field' arrival took place when John Alexander came as treasurer. He was a necessary calming influence in the routinely volatile committee meetings:

Phil Neal, ex-Liverpool and England (standing third from the right) joins Alex (standing on the right) and the West Allotment Committee to celebrate success

"I was summoned to a meeting once and told I couldn't play Chaffey and Milburn in the same team. I told the committee that I would listen and respect their views but when it came to a management decision if I felt they could play together they did. One of the problems was that they were inclined to be too critical of their own players. If anyone else did it they would tear their backs off but on match days their passion clouded their judgement."

After five years as manager of West Allotment Alex came to the realisation that he had taken his players as far as he could. He was honest enough to know that they were capable of producing more but that they had become too used to him, so he relinquished the manager's role and joined the committee:

> "I let the managers and coaches do the work on the pitch and the training-ground and I went out and spotted players. One of the first was a goalkeeper who was with Whitley Bay; Whitley had snapped up Simon Smith when he was released by Newcastle, so I signed David Marshall and he has gone on to play over 600 games for us. He's been a fantastic servant."

Ray Taylor managed the side for a couple of seasons, then Les Jackson, a workaholic like Alex in the West Allotment cause, took over. After Les Jackson, Richard Percy was appointed manager and he lifted the club to a new level of professionalism. He brought Micky Cairns back as his assistant and it was during this period that West Allotment began to make their reputation in the FA Vase. Alex describes himself as the third point on a triangle with Richard and Micky, claiming with justification that they produced a Northern Alliance side which was as good as any in the Northern league:

> "All our managers have been enthusiastic but none more so than Richard Percy. He did his homework on the opposition and Micky was the aggressive coach, while Richard was the mild-mannered, arm-around-the-shoulder type. We played Willington once and I told our lads that their keeper was always off his line; we won the game with a 30-yard lob over the keeper's head. Little things like that helped and gave you a lift."

Richard Percy had good players at West Allotment; John Kiddie, David Biley, Ian Chater who could play in goal or centre-forward and Ian Curle who was a key defender. Richard's organisation was outstanding and he could change his formation from 4-2-4 to 4-3-3 with equal facility. However, work commitments began to take their toll and despite constant chivvying from Mr Smailes, Richard resigned after one year in charge to be replaced by Daz Ridley and Mickey Richardson:

> "You wouldn't have imagined Daz as a manager in view of his antics as a player but his name kept cropping up among the players when I asked for their opinion, so I met him in Tynemouth club and discussed it with him. It probably changed his life. His reputation changed from reprobate and scally to responsible person and his attitude altered to such an extent that he now has his own business. We tried to get Ian Watts and Wilfie Waite but Daz turned out to be superb."

Daz Ridley became hugely successful as West Allotment's manager, winning both the double and the treble, while Alex continued in his role as guide and helper:

> "I had learned things and I helped other people to learn things. I grafted really hard to maintain the West Allotment standard and I do get upset when people criticise the club because of their success."

Daz stepped down as manager and was replaced by Davie Taylor, a cultured centre-half who had played for the club for years and whose appointment highlighted the theme of continuity which has been a hallmark of West Allotment.

One of the highlights of Davie Taylor's period of tenure, during which Alex produced another young professional, Neil MacDonald of

Newcastle, to help with the coaching, was a Northumberland Senior cup-tie against Newcastle United:

"It was a great opportunity for us and I was determined to see it was done properly. We planned it in every detail, involving the police and St John's Ambulance. I had the idea of buying in stewards from the company which stewarded St. James's Park and we even had a minibus to take the players the 300 yards from the dressing rooms to the pitch. The organisation was a triumph for the committee. We lost the game before a crowd of over 2000 but the Newcastle people were very complimentary and it was not only the start of a good relationship, but evidence for the older committee members that the club's resurgence was complete. I'd come a long way from the Seahorse."

West Allotment lost the league title that season in a play-off against Seaton Terrace, who were managed by Ken Scott (later to become a hugely successful manager at Allotment). The first match was a draw and the league ordered the replay to take place on Easter Monday night, a decision which caused Alex's hackles to rise as he thought the players were entitled to their Bank Holiday. A team including Micky Storey, John Fitzpatrick, John Kiddie and Keith 'Chalky' Woods (known to Alex as Eddie Murphy the second) took on Terrace and Micky Chilton equalised for Allotment in the last minute. The game went into extra time and Terrace scored the winner off their centre-forward's shin. It was a bitter blow and there was a lot of agonising by manager and players through the close season.

When Alex resigned as manager of the club he embarked on another activity which has had an indelible impact on his life. Through his friendship with Ray Kennedy he attended Liverpool matches home and away on a regular basis and when Ray informed the manager, Bob Paisley, and the chief scout Geoff Twentyman of Alex's non-league involvement he was invited to become North-East scout for what was then the best club side in the world. He began by watching non-league players and reporting back and the job has developed to the extent that he now assesses the opposition at Premiership level and produces complex and detailed reports for the Anfield club on the playing styles, strengths and weaknesses of opponents.

It was as a consequence of his Liverpool connection that Alex was responsible for orchestrating what he describes as the greatest night in West Allotment's history. He had always produced top-class guests to make the presentations at end-of-season functions, including Peter Beardsley, Paul Gascoigne and the current chief scout at Liverpool, Ron Yeats:

"Ron Yeats was put up at a hotel, then I collected him and took him to the mansion at Backworth. There were 130 people there and they had paid the comedian off because he was crap. Big Ron stood up and did a spot off the cuff which brought the house down. He turned a potential disaster into an excellent night."

Alex's triumph was to follow. He had asked Kenny Dalglish to come up and present the medals if Allotment won the league and Kenny said he would be pleased to come irrespective. When John Jackson rang him with the date he said his availability depended on Blackburn Rovers, whom he was then managing, being involved in the play-offs, which would delay his family holiday. Thankfully, that scenario came about and Kenny, turning down the opportunity to stay in a hotel and arranging for his wife to drive him up to save the club money, met Alex and made his way to the venue:

West Allotment celebration night, with guest Kenny Dalglish

"Apart from John Jackson and me only John Alexander knew what was going on and when we arrived and John introduced him the place went wild. It was our greatest ever night. Kenny

Dalglish is much maligned but as a friend he is tops."

There followed a period of transition for West

Allotment with John Kiddie acting as player-manager for a season-and-a-half and recruiting young talent such as Tony Woodhouse. Ken Scott then became manager, and under his shrewd tutelage the team continued to dominate the Northern Alliance, and indeed Ken Scott's record as manager surpasses the achievements of all his predecessors — no mean feat. Alex Smailes for his part has ceased to have any official role at the club, and after close involvement for 21 years the decision to quit was a sad one:

"I had to do it because of my growing involvement with Liverpool, but West Allotment is still in my heart and I still manage to help Ken Scott whenever I can."

Alex surprised virtually everyone in local non-league football circles when he turned from poacher to gamekeeper by becoming involved with the Northumberland Football Association. A constant and vociferous irritant to officialdom, his decision to cross the road came from a realisation that he could fight the cause of players more effectively from inside the system than he could be banging on its doors, and he is now a respected member of the NFA Council, representing the east division with Ted Ilderton. One of his motives in joining the governing body of the game north of the Tyne was his belief that its balance was wrong:

"It was dominated by referees and Sunday morning representatives, but it's Saturday clubs that set the standards. Saturday and Sunday teams have the same voting power, which can't be right. For instance Blyth Waterloo put their nets up at 10:30 on a Sunday morning, play their game and go home at 12:30, full stop, while Blyth Spartans have to have floodlights, stewarding, a match programme, a referees' room and covered access to the pitch, yet they have the same power. The right thing should be done."

Alex responds to the accusation that he is a players' man by regarding that as a virtue rather than a weakness, and goes on cite what he regards as his proudest achievement as an NFA official as evidence that he takes a broad view. He succeeded in persuading his colleagues that their award for meritorious service should be extended to include all who deserved it on merit and not remain limited to club chairmen, secretaries and treasurers:

"I have tried to represent the fact that committee men and players are important. You can't have too many good committee men."

Alex's commitment to Liverpool FC means that he is frequently required to attend major games in the Premiership, but he is still a non-league man who likes nothing better than to return from a big match to watch a game in the Northern League or the Alliance to remind him of where he came from and where he belongs; to meet the people at the grass roots and to hear the crack.

This intensely loyal man, who spent 20 years in official capacities at West Allotment, has been associated with Liverpool for 20 years, and has worked for the same employer for 35 years, has upset a lot of people along the way, because there is no middle ground with Alex Smailes.

His willingness to help people is limitless; whether it's organising a lifetime pass to the Sands Club for George Courteney or a trip to Anfield to meet his idol Bill Shankly for Stan Nixon. In short he is a fixer. It was Alex who stepped in, for instance, before the 1998 FA Cup semi-final when Newcastle United wanted a friendly to test Duncan Ferguson's fitness. Alex rang all the West Allotment players and arranged for them to be at Newcastle's training ground in Chester le Street,

Northumberland FA Officials — left to right: Sid Johnson, Roland Maughan, Alex Smailes, Alan Wright and Les Todd.

and when the game was leaked to the press, it was Alex who organised everyone to go to St. James's Park to play the game behind closed doors. He made sure the players swapped shirts afterwards and saw to it that John Fitzpatrick, who had been substituted, received Stuart Pearce's shirt. He also arranged for the club to receive a shirt signed by the Newcastle players which they could raffle to boost their funds.

Alex has close friendships with countless ex-players; Kenny Dalglish, Phil Neal, Ian Rush, Graeme Souness and many more. The reason? He's intensely loyal, tenacious and totally honest. He's also incredibly conscientious; take a look at one of the match reports he produces for Liverpool if you doubt either his work-rate or his knowledge of the game. He upsets people, does Alex Smailes, but he doesn't let them down; he delivers.

PAUL WALKER

Big balls in winter, small ones in summer.

Young Paul (seated centre) captains his school team

Paul Walker was arguably the most skilful midfield player to adorn the non-league scene in the north-east of England in his era. It's probably in the genes because his father, George, was steeped in the game — and indeed it was as a result of Mr. Walker's role as north-east scout for Aston Villa that one of Paul's early opportunities arose to sample the game at professional level. Young Paul Walker played his schoolboy football for Hetton Lyons school in County Durham and graduated to St Aidan's Grammar in Sunderland, making regular trips to Villa Park in the school holidays. However he also had the opportunity to sign apprentice professional forms with Sunderland, and when it came to making a choice between Roker Park and Villa Park he chose the former, not predominantly for football reasons but because he was reluctant to relinquish his other love; playing cricket in the summer for Hetton Lyons:

"A daft Scotsman called Ray Yeomans was in charge of the Sunderland apprentices; lads like Tony Maggiore, Dave and Tommy Callaghan, Davie Rutter and Peter Stronach. In those days the lives of the professionals and the apprentices were totally separate. I only had one pair of boots — you had to buy your own, and in the close season you would work your bollocks off on the training ground then go back to Roker Park. Sometimes you had to wash the chairman's car, and one of our jobs was to scrape the birds' shite off the seats in the stand, but no sooner had you done it than the birds shat on them again."

Paul's spell at Roker Park came to an end when he was one of 12 apprentices released by Bob Stokoe, and it was a particularly disappointing blow for a lad harbouring dreams of playing for his local side. Trials with Grimsby Town followed, then an opportunity to join Hull City, where his father was now scouting. He enjoyed his 18 months at Hull, who were managed by the respected former West Bromwich Albion defender John Kaye. He was in the company of several players from his home environment; goalkeeper Eddie Blackburn from Easington Lane, Davie Gibson from Houghton, and the current Sky TV pundit and former Arsenal winger Brian Marwood, who hailed from Seaham and who according to Paul couldn't win a place in Hull's reserve team!

"I played four reserve games and scored four goals from left-back. It was a superb time and I found it easy to settle due to the north-east connection. Plus it was only an hour-and-a-half's drive from home when I wanted to play cricket. Cricket has always been a great love and I played the two games back to back until I was 42. I would train for football twice a week and go to the winter nets; I was never in the house. That's probably why I've been married three times. My present wife makes the teas so I'm probably safe, though it took me five years to persuade her."

During his contented spell at Hull City Football Club Paul was sent for a loan spell at Doncaster Rovers, who were managed by Stan Anderson. Unfortunately he was soured by the fact that he first learned about the move through the newspapers and he took it badly. Billy Bremner had been a recent recruit to the club and he advised him to go for the experience, but despite the fact that he was doing well it was a turning-point in his burgeoning career:

"I went back to Hull and my landlady thought I had left the club and there was no room for me at the digs so I had to sleep in the car for three nights. I was fed up and I came home. Looking back it was a bad mistake because I was doing well, but I was only 21 and I was engaged, so I gave it up and came back to get married."

His decision to turn his back on the professional game, in which he clearly had a future, was a particularly disappointing one for his father; the two of them were close in sporting terms, playing cricket together in the summer, and his father had been an important influence and guide in this football career. However, the decision was made and life moved on. Paul was only home a week when his brother Gerald arranged for him to play for Terry Kirkbride at Horden Colliery Welfare in the Northern League. He stayed there for three years, until the club were excluded from the league because their lights were inadequate; the consequence for Paul was a move to Scarborough:

"Gerry Donohue took me there with Gerry Hogan and Brian Magee, and Harry Dunn was there as well. Gerry was a hard taskmaster and that was the toughest pre-season I ever had. Scarborough was a very good and professional club and they had some excellent players but I didn't stay long; I was in and out of the side and Jimmy Turney and Jackie Marks were putting a lot of pressure on me to go to Blyth, so I went to Croft Park and in the six years I was there we won the league five times."

Paul Walker's midfield skills made him a popular figure at Blyth and he had a powerful champion in Jackie Marks. Indeed when Paul left the Spartans to join Newcastle Blue Star at the end of that six-year spell and returned to play for them in the semi-final of the FA Trophy, Jackie Marks recommended him to the manager of the England non-league team who was at the game; a recommendation which was to bear fruit. One of the great characters on the playing side at Blyth was Ian 'Archie' Mutrie, who was Paul's great friend and who invited him to tea after one match:

"I sat down at the dining table and he asked me if I wanted steak or mince. Naturally I opted for the steak, so he brought me a steak pie and had the mince pie himself."

Paul's spell at Blue Star, although it lasted only a season and was punctuated with friction between himself and chairman Billy Dryden and manager Colin Richardson, was nevertheless highly successful:

"Blue Star never won as many trophies in a season as they did that year but I never got mine yet. I'm sure Colin Richardson's got them displayed on top of his sewing machine at home."

After that season of great success but off-the-field disenchantment, Paul returned to his first Northern League club Horden, who were now happily restored to the fold, and he inspired them to a sensational victory over Blyth Spartans in the final of the league cup. That triumph was built around a tremendous midfield consisting of Paul, Davie Robson and Graham Hedley:

"It was a fantastic result; a great example of the colliery lads coming good. The top clubs thought they were better than us so it was particularly satisfying."

Paul returned to Blyth Spartans and during his second season the words of Jackie Marks paid dividends when he was selected to play for the England non-league side against Wales at Merthyr Tydfil:

"My father drove for seven hours to watch me then drove back again for another seven hours. It was a weird feeling standing in an England shirt listening to the national anthem; the Welsh crowd were calling me a fat English bastard but it didn't matter because I couldn't understand Welsh."

The cap against Wales was followed by selection for a four-team tournament in Scotland the following season involving the host nation, Holland and Italy. It was an opportunity to train and play with the cream of non-league talent as well as a great chance to join with the scousers in taking the piss out of the cockneys! The southern players had the last laugh, however, when the conversation got around to money. They were talking in terms of £25,000 signing-on fees and BMWs and Paul was playing for Blyth for £50 a week — a perfect illustration of the north/south divide in non-league football:

Paul (front row, second left) in the England non-league team

Paul's international adventure continued the year after he left Blyth to join Bishop Auckland, when he was invited to join the famous Middlesex Wanderers on their close-season tour of Indonesia. The long 21-hour flight, with stops in Malaysia and Saudi Arabia, was a potential downside, but the free beer on the plane made it tolerable! Malaysia, of course, is an equatorial country and routinely has 30 degrees of humidity, so even with an eight o'clock kick-off the playing conditions were hot and debilitating:

"Actually I told them I got ten bob a week, a bag of fish and chips and a go at the manager's wife. Seriously though, I'm proud of the fact that I was probably the last Northern League player to represent England at non-league level. When you consider the number of people playing football in the north-east that's not a bad achievement."

The honour of playing for his country brought Paul to the attention of clubs outside the region, and among the opportunities which came his way was an offer from Jimmy McIlroy to sign for Nuneaton Borough, but again his desire to play local cricket was a determining factor, and he was quite content with his combined earnings from his football and his day job.

"We had a full-back who went on the overlap and he was so exhausted he couldn't get back. They had buckets of ice on the touch line with towels in to help us keep cool. The country was a place of amazing contrasts; one street would be like a scene from 'Dallas' and the next would be slums. The degradation was awful. We were going over this bridge on the coach and the river below was the colour of charcoal. I saw this bloke having a shite in the water and a few yards away another one was cleaning his teeth. I'm a cockly person and I don't mind admitting I threw up when I saw that."

The Wanderers were involved in a four-team tournament with sides from Poland, China and Indonesia itself, and Paul was particularly impressed by the quality of the one-touch football produced by the Poles; it was one of several memories of a brilliant experience despite the intolerable combination of heat and humidity.

The playing career of Paul Walker is littered with highlights, the next of which came in 1989, by which time he was playing for Whitley Bay, and he had the unforgettable experience of being in the side which defeated Preston North End in the second round of the FA Cup:

"Sixteen lads from Hetton Lyons cricket club came through to watch the match and on the way they bought 16 cheap plastic footballs, cut them in half, turned them inside out and put them on their heads to imitate me. They stood beside one of the corner flags and the first time I went towards them they all shouted 'baldy' and pointed at their heads. I was doubled up."

The game itself was a triumph for Whitley who won 2-0, and an equal triumph for Paul Walker who imposed himself on the opposition from the outset and ran the game. He remembers vividly being spoken to after the game by Sir Tom Finney in the bar and being told by the great man that it was obvious he had a professional background and was to be complimented on his performance:

"It was a great moment, and that Whitley Bay side was one of the best I played in. My only disappointment was that the players went their separate ways after the game. It was such a special occasion we should have spent the night enjoying it together."

From Whitley Bay Paul rejoined Bishop Auckland for a couple of seasons before moving to Seaham Red Star for four years. Billy Cruddas at Durham City had tried to sign him for years and after his Seaham stint he eventually went to Ferens Park, but he cricked his back playing cricket and was injured for five months:

Paul in action for Whitley Bay against Preston in the FA Cup

"Billy was foaming. He called me all the fat bastards under the sun, but there was nothing I could do."

Summers continued to be devoted to cricket, principally with Hetton Lyons whom he had joined as a seven-year-old — at which age he made his debut for the under-18 side, scoring four runs and taking a catch. That early promise flourished and he had spells as club professional at Eppleton Colliery Welfare and Seaham Park:

"Seaham were known as the grins because everyone drank Federation LCL lager which is powerful stuff and we all ended up grinning. When I joined them a bandy-legged old codger called Jackie Thirkell, who had wanted me to play for them for years, said 'we've finally got you; put your car keys behind the bar, you're drinking with me'."

Back to football, and in his late thirties, Paul began the demanding task of combining playing with management, first with Chris 'Scatter' Copeland at Seaham Red Star. It was an enjoyable experience which gave him a different perspective on the game. Standing in the bar after training one night he overheard a conversation between two of his players, Michael Robinson, who was a joker, and Michael Parkinson, whom Paul categorised as a 'temperamental superstar.' During their conversation Parkinson claimed that there were no circumstances in which the manager would drop him from the team:

Paul today — 'The icing on the cake'

"That weekend we had a derby match and when I announced the team he was substitute. I did it to show him that no one was indispensable. He wasn't very happy and it didn't help when Robinson gave him all five of the substitutes' track suits because it was a cold day. Kevin Wolfe and Gary McDonald were jokers as well and they kept shouting over to the bench to ask him if he was warm enough."

Finally, Paul had a year as manager at Durham City, but he found it frustrating because he wasn't able to influence matters on the field and he found it difficult to adjust to the fact that players weren't capable of doing the things he had been able to do himself. So he is now enjoying his first break from the game of football since he was a 15-year-old. He is still heavily involved in cricket at Hetton Lyons who are now operating successfully in the Durham Senior League. The family tradition is safe as well; Paul's 12-year-old son Michael — a great wrestling fan and self-styled WWF minder for Kevin Wolfe — plays at Hetton, and his 16-year-old nephew Stuart is already attracting the interest of Durham. The sporting future of the Walker dynasty appears to be in secure hands.

BILLY WRIGHT

Scourge of Goalkeepers

Billy in his prime

Billy Wright terrified goalkeepers. At 6'2" and 14 stones he was a powerful physical specimen and as a centre-forward he was possessed of raw courage and sheer determination. If the ball was there to be won Billy would win it irrespective of any obstacle which might have stood in his way, and that included goalkeepers.

Billy's reputation as a fearsome centre-forward was made during the 11 years he spent with Whitley Bay from 1962 to 1973, having been

Early days at Whitley Bay FC

spotted by the late Arthur Clark, then Bay's Secretary, playing for Wallsend St. Columba's Under-19 side against Wallsend Corinthians in the final of the Percy Hedley Cup at the North Road ground in Wallsend. St. Columba's won the trophy thanks to an extra-time Billy Wright goal. Charlie Crowe, Newcastle United FA Cup hero of the early 1950s, was coming to the end of his tenure as manager of Whitley Bay when Billy signed, and into Charlie's shoes stepped another ex-professional called Bobby Keen — whose major eccentricity was to wear his track suit on top of his suit, collar and tie:

"I took one look at him and thought that cannot be right. All he wanted to do in training was play five-a-side and I remember once our goalkeeper Roy Coates, who was 6'8", leaning against his goal-post in training wearing his tracksuit over his suit and smoking his pipe. You couldn't take Bobby seriously."

In those days of the early sixties Whitley Bay was not a football club whose players and officials came from the same kind of working-class background as Billy Wright. In the main they were professional and semi-professional people such as teachers, businessman and salesmen, and they found Billy something of a culture shock;

"When I first turned up I'd been at work in the shipyards. I went straight from work to training in me boots and overalls, with holes in me socks and me haversack over me shoulder. I was keen to impress so I went running around like a lunatic whacking everybody, and I could hear them saying, keep away from him, he's a nutter. I was careful not to kick then too much, though, because a lot of them were civil servants and sales reps and I knew I would be tapping them for lifts in their cars. The directors were all blazer men; wealthy people."

In those early days Billy was about as far from today's pampered players as it is possible to conceive:

"I finished work at the shipyards at twenty to five and I had to catch the quarter past five train from Wallsend, so I ran the mile and a bit from the yards to Daisy Hill where I lived, picked up a training bag and an egg sandwich the wife had made, and ran back to the station. I'd done half my training before I got to Hillheads."

Billy didn't establish himself in the Whitley Bay side for a while, and after playing in a friendly against Wallsend Corinthians he was approached by Davey Davidson, the manager of Ashington, and offered £2 to play for them the following Wednesday night. Davey went through the proper channels and Whitley Bay gave permission for him to play; it was a big step up from junior football to the Northern Counties League for a raw 19-year-old, but Billy had a big heart and an appetite for hard work and he scored two goals on his Ashington debut.

After the game Davidson offered him £4 to play again on Saturday and Billy, already married and earning less than £8:50 a week in the shipyards, was happy to accept. Once again he scored two goals and after training at Whitley Bay the following Tuesday night Davey Davidson met him again, this time offering him £6 to turn out again. The following week Arthur Clark and one of the Whitley bay directors called at Billy's house and reminded him of his obligation to Whitley Bay, with whom he was registered. They agreed to pay him £6 a week but after training the following week Davey Davidson was waiting for him in his car:

"The best I can do is £8 a game. It's more than anybody else is getting and it's in your hand."

So Ashington won the short-term battle for Billy's services and that season he scored more than 30 goals for Davidson's team. However, there was a lot of travelling involved in the Northern Counties League and the following season Whitley Bay came back with an offer which he accepted:

"They paid me £6 or £7 a week, which was canny money. I was already married with a kid and we were living with my mother so I wanted to get a few quid together to find the deposit on a mortgage. Besides, getting to training was even worse at Ashington. I had to go through the same routine to get the train from Wallsend to Whitley Bay then run another mile from the station to Davey Davidson's chiropodist shop near the Spanish City."

It still took a while before Billy Wright became a permanent fixture in the Whitley Bay side. Kenny Grant was usually preferred, and on one occasion Billy scored a hat trick against Spennymoor United but was still left out the following week.

Bay were a useful side with the likes of Brian Oakley and Neil Walton playing for them, but too many of the players were at the veteran stage for them to be a really successful outfit. However, things were about to change with the arrival of a new manager. Bobby Owen ran things in a professional manner and he transformed the whole club. The likes of Kenny Sloan and Billy were still in and out of the team, but even though Bobby Owen introduced better players to Hillheads, early results were erratic, so by working hard in training and making the most of opportunities when they did come along Billy eventually established himself:

"I think it was partly because I wasn't a suit-and-tie merchant that it took me so long. There were little cliques of three or four here and there and I sometimes used to think about some of them, 'what a stuck up bastard, I'll make him squeal in training.' I soon learned that they were all tough players in the Northern League. We went to Stanley one day and they had a player called Jackie Wilkinson: he was only 5'2" and he was a cracking little player but he was a nasty little pig. Stanley won a corner and Jackie Wilkinson hit our keeper Roy Coates, who was 6'8". Roy ended up in the back of the net and little Jackie scored from the corner then he turned to Roy and said; 'Hello Roy, how are you keeping?' We were howling."

Inevitably, when next the two sides met it was a physical battle, one which Whitley won 2-0. After the game one of the Stanley players, Dougie Raine, punched Billy in the back as the players were leaving the field, then, realising the error of his ways, he ran to the dressing room, locked himself in and stood shaking with trepidation while his team-mates and Billy tried to open the door.

Billy Wright was proving more than capable of coping with those 'tough players' in the Northern League and was establishing his own reputation as a 'tough bastard.' Goalkeepers in particular felt the full force of his physical presence. In his own words he,

"put the fear of God into goalkeepers. Physical contact was much more a part of the game then and some keepers like Billy Patrick wouldn't go anywhere near me. Jimmy Goundry played for Tow Law at the time and once he miskicked a clearance and kicked me in the balls. After

the game he said: 'I kicked him in the balls and he never went down. That's it; I'm signing for Whitley Bay' — and he did."

Billy's speciality was to harass the goalkeeper as he attempted to clear the ball, standing a couple of yards in front of his man and throwing himself in front of the attempted clearance. This often saw him block the ball with some part of his anatomy and enabled him to score from the loose ball.

There was one goalkeeper who was unlikely to be intimidated by Billy's physical proximity and he was Bishop Auckland's England Amateur international, Harry Sharratt, and Billy was warned by Ian Tindale not to get involved with him:

"He's good. He'll make a fool of you. Well, we drew with them in a cup-tie and brought them back to our place and sure enough the first couple of times I closed him down he bounced the ball over my head, caught it and cleared upfield. He was taking the mickey and I just said each time; 'that was great Harry.' The third time he tried it he dropped the ball and I passed it to Bobby Kane who scored. I just turned to Sharratt again and said: 'that was great Harry.' What a sickener!"

Like all strikers Billy depended on good service and he has a particular fondness in this regard for Kenny Sloan:

"Underrated. I loved him as a player, a friend, and a drinking partner. Still do. Then there were wingers like Johnny Gatens and Gordon Lamb. The service was first-class."

Whitley Bay had become a very good side under the guidance of Bobby Owen. They attracted crowds of over 1000 and Billy Wright became a cult figure with his goalscoring prowess, his total

The FA Amateur Cup Semi-Final at Roker Park

commitment in every game, and his fun and games with goalkeepers. It was a mutual thing: the crowd loved Billy and he loved them. Success included twice reaching the semi-finals of the old FA Amateur Cup; the first time against Hendon at Roker Park before a crowd of 18,000:

"They were the first southern side we had played, so we knew what to expect when we played them again in the semi-final. That first time we played them down at their place you could tell they were a wealthy club. They were bankrolled by Billy Butlin — the holiday camp man. They had a great ground and the players were up to £50 a game. To be fair they were a smashing side and the first time we played them they destroyed us with their pace and movement and their one-touch football. It was so good you could see why they were on £50 and we were on a fiver. They were in decent jobs as well so they didn't need to think about turning pro. The

semi-final was different, though. We outclassed them but we couldn't score. We conceded a goal in the first minute and we were 2-0 down in half an hour but we pulled one back and after that we played 'shooting in' but we couldn't score. We were all in tears at full-time, but we'd had a great cup run."

Most teams prefer a home draw in cup competitions but many of the Whitley Bay players preferred to be drawn away so that they could enjoy a weekend in a good hotel at the club's expense :

We once had to play a team in Leeds in an Amateur Cup tie on New Year's Day and we travelled the day before. Arthur Clark booked us into a temperance hotel for New Year's Eve! Brian Oakley and I had no money; we were waiting for our match fee, so we borrowed ten bob each off Jack Tait, the Chairman, and we

Billy (far left) on target for Whitley Bay at Hillheads

were straight out of the door, We went into the dance hall next door for a couple of pints and later on these birds invited us to a party so we got on the bus and went with them. When we arrived there was no party and we were left high and dry about 15 miles from the hotel. We flagged down this car, and somebody up there must have been looking out for us because the driver was a Geordie and he took us back to the hotel. When he dropped us off the poor lad reversed his car into a wall. Next morning Bobby Owen went mad and the directors told him to leave us out of the side. At 1:30 he came into our room and said: 'You're both playing and if either of you let me down again this afternoon I'll bloody chin you.' We both had blinders; I scored and we beat them 2-1."

One aspect of life on away trips where Billy felt compelled to impose his wishes was the issue of pre-match lunches. The usual practice was for the team to have a light lunch of scrambled egg on toast, but at home Billy was used to a Saturday lunch of fish and chips with three slices of bread and a cup of tea. He made his point and from then his away-day meal consisted of steak.

Whitley Bay's second FA Amateur Cup semi-final was against Sutton, and Billy still contends that the Football Association contributed to their second failure to reach Wembley. North Shields had also reached the semi-final stage and there was agreement that whichever of the two came out of the hat first would play their game in the

North-East. In the event, Whitley were drawn first but their match was scheduled for St. Andrew's, Birmingham while Shields played Skelmersdale in the North-East:

"It was daft to play a game between a northern team and a southern team in the Midlands. We would rather have gone to their place. We were disheartened to have to travel there and we had no real support. There were only 5000 in that big ground and there was no atmosphere. The other thing was, we picked the wrong team. We had an outstanding full-back in Michael Ritchie but he wasn't picked and they had a pacy winger who did the damage against us, and we went out. North Shields never gave him a kick in the final and they won the cup. Whitley Bay against North Shields would have been some final, though."

Actually, Ken Walshaw, long-time North Shields manager, tried several times to persuade Billy to sign for him. On one occasion he even put a blank cheque in front of him and invited to fill in the amount himself, but Billy wasn't tempted; he loved the spirit at Whitley Bay and revelled in his popularity with the Bay supporters. Other teams recognised his ability and he had opportunities to play in the South of England and South Africa, but as a young married man with two children he was reluctant to uproot his family. Recognition also came his way in the shape of selection for the North against the South in a representative match and an invitation to tour Asia with the famous Middlesex Wanderers which, sadly, injury prevented him from accepting.

Eventually, Billy's time at Whitley Bay came to an end. At the age of 32 Bobby Owen took the view that he was past his prime. He was by now coaching the Whitley Bay reserve team and even though he was brought back into the senior side towards the end of the season when an injury crisis erupted, he was destined for the reserves again the following season, so, feeling that he wasn't wanted, he went to play for Jackie Marks at Ashington, where once again Stanley FC figured in a bizarre incident:

"The snow was bleaching down there in November and it was a freezing cold day. Bobby Kane went past their centre-half and scored and the defender never moved. He was still rooted to the spot when Bobby ran past him again on his way back to the centre-spot. The poor bugger was so cold he couldn't move and the trainer had to come on and see to him before he froze to death. We were all freezing, but the team bath there was tiny; it only held three people at a time and if you were last you were getting washed in mud."

Billy's return to Ashington wasn't greeted with universal approval. The dissenting voice was that of Eddie Nesbitt, the goalkeeper, who had been on the receiving end of Billy's robust challenges on many occasions. When Jackie Marks took Billy into the dressing room the keeper yelled:

"What's that bastard doing here? Get him out."

His protests continued until Jackie pointed out that Billy was now an Ashington player and past differences must be resolved. After the game Billy bought Eddie Nesbitt a pint of lager, a gesture which began the thawing process in their relationship. A team which included good players such as Brian Pringle and Tommy Dixon as well as Nesbitt and Wright was beginning to meet with success. Syd Bell, recently released by West Bromwich Albion and still young in experience, was placed in charge for an upcoming Amateur Cup tie at Marine. It was an ill-considered decision which upset some of the players, who gave Syd

Bell a hard time and threatened not to play. Syd turned to Billy Wright as the senior player for guidance and Billy pointed out to the players that the young man had been pitchforked into a situation not of his own making and which he hadn't the experience to handle. He emphasised the importance of the Amateur Cup and the need to pull together. On the Saturday morning two of the players were injured during a training session on Southport beach and Les Mutrie, who had said he wouldn't play, was selected:

> "I asked him why he was there if he didn't want to play and told him to take his chance. He got stuck in and had a cracking game which really launched his career. We won 2-1 and I scored the winner two minutes from time."

Superstition is a powerful influence on many footballers, and Billy Wright believes it was superstition which cost him his third and final opportunity of an appearance in an FA Amateur Cup final at Wembley. The man involved was his old adversary, now his room-mate, Eddie Nesbitt who had used the same pair of tie-ups in every round of the competition but when he came to assemble his kit for the semi-final one of them was missing, and this he regarded as an omen of ill-fortune. During the game he fumbled the kind of cross he normally caught as a matter of routine and in trying to retrieve the situation he damaged his shoulder. Refusing to leave the field, he was restricted by his injury and conceded three goals. After the game he swore:

> "It was the tie-ups, Billy, it was the tie-ups."

So Billy Wright's FA Amateur Cup quest ended with a third semi-final defeat. Marking him in that Ashington match was the Bishop Stortford centre-half Roy Sleep:

> "He was tough as teak and he had missed out twice before as well. After the game he bought me a pint. It was third time lucky for him and although I was disappointed for myself I had given him some real thumpings and I was pleased for him."

The following season Billy took over as manager of Ashington and very quickly created an excellent young team containing the likes of Bobby Graham, Keith Tweddle, Brian Pringle and Ian Crumplin. He was building a side capable of competing with the Blyth Spartans, the Bishop Aucklands and the Spennymoor Uniteds, including in his team several young players he found in junior football, and with Kenny Sloan as his assistant he was beginning to put Ashington back on the football map. He knew the game and he understood the value of good team spirit. Many players still speak highly of Billy Wright and the opportunities he provided for them at Ashington. Unfortunately, one of the club's four directors persuaded his colleagues that he could produce just as good a side using players from the Ashington area, and Billy was sacked. In the view of many people that decision marked the beginning of a decline in Ashington Football club's fortunes from which they have never recovered.

There is further irony in the fact that earlier Billy had rejected the opportunity to manage Newcastle Blue Star out of loyalty to his young Ashington side. Blue Star went on to win the FA Vase at Wembley and Billy Wright got the sack. He went on to manage Marine Park and to coach successfully at Bedlington for Bobby Graham before retiring.

All the while, Billy had enjoyed a hugely successful parallel playing career in Sunday football playing for Ray Donaldson's redoubtable Birds Nest side, which won every division of the

Successful days at Whitley Bay

North East Sunday League. They played their football at Harbottle Park, which was known in local parlance as the Aztec Stadium because it was an ancient ruin, and they were phenomenally successful. They had a large and fanatical following and Billy was every bit as idolised by the Birds Nest supporters as he was by those at Hillheads. He gives a lot of the credit for his success in Sunday football to a great winger called Peter 'Lob' Stephenson:

"Lob was a fantastic player. He used to say 'divvent jump, I'll put the ball on your heed.' If he could have left the Brown Ale bottle alone he would have been a world-beater."

Billy has retained his interest in Sunday League football and is now the referees' representative on the league management committee. He refereed for 20 years after ending his playing career, reaching the Football League list:

"I was a good referee but my knees are knackered. If you can find me two new knees I'll take it up again."

There was one particularly proud moment in Billy's refereeing career which provides a fitting note on which to close. His son, also Billy, is an international footballer with over 20 caps for New Zealand, and on the occasion of a friendly match between the New Zealand national side and Newcastle United at St. James's Park the FA had the presence of mind to appoint Billy as the fourth match official:

Billy today — still ready for action

"John Watson, who was Billy's old teacher, was the referee that night and I was in the stand hoping to see the lad score a goal. Some people who were sitting behind me recognised me and as I turned to acknowledge them Billy scored — I missed it, but I'm very proud of him. He's got two of the three coaching badges he needs to coach in the Premiership and he's still playing top-class football at the age of 34. He lives in Australia now and he plays in the Australian Premier League. They treat him like a god over there."

The Wright dynasty appears to be in safe hands, and Billy himself is still making an important contribution; for the last few years he has been coaching the Northumberland County Under-18 side with George Ormond.

He earns his living driving his taxi on Tyneside, so if you're a goalkeeper the next time you're in a taxi take a good look at the driver, and be prepared to take evasive action!

RAY YOUNG

Fried Rice and Leather Handbags.

Ray Young — Here and now

Ray Young's early playing days involved the kind of do-it-yourself basics which many North-East youngsters experienced in their desire to play football. Beginning as a 12-year-old with Peter Kirkley's Willington Quay and Howdon Boys Club sides he helped to carry the goal-posts a quarter of a mile through a housing estate to the

Meldon Close pitch in Willington Quay. It was a common occurrence for women to push their prams across the pitch — and the games had to be held up to accommodate them. These distractions didn't deter Ray, however, and he progressed through the boys' club ranks until he was spotted as a 15-year-old and given trials by

Middlesbrough and Carlisle United before going to Preston North End:

"Sir Stanley Matthews had been to the house when he was manager of Port Vale, but I didn't like his approach so I went to Preston. Gordon Milne's father, Jimmy Milne, was the manager. I was fifteen and I cleaned Howard Kendall's boots. Archie Gemmell also joined the club; a lovely man and awfully fit. Ernie Hannigan was one of the great characters there; we got paid on Thursdays and he would come into the boot room on Friday morning claiming he had a pull and couldn't train, but he was always OK to play on the Saturday."

Ray found himself well capable of coping with the playing standard at Preston and compared playing at the North Road training ground with playing with his mates in the back lane back home in Wallsend. It wasn't long, however, before he found himself in trouble. Ray didn't begin drinking until he was 18, but nevertheless went out with some team-mates one night and became involved in an altercation in a local bar. They were taken to the local police station and although a telephone call to the football club resulted in no charges being brought, he was fined two weeks wages for being on licensed premises after ten o'clock on a Friday night:

"A week's wages in 1965 was £11:50 and your digs were paid for."

Despite his brush with authority things went well for Ray at Preston and a promising career seemed likely, but the youngster soon became disenchanted:

"I loved football, but not the professional game. I was taught how to look after myself on the field and I learned all the tricks of the trade. One pro told me I had no friends on the training pitch because I had to 'want their shirts' and they were after mine. The professional game wasn't what I had envisioned football to be. I played in every outfield position at Preston, which was a fine education, but I think lesser players than me made more progress. Anyway, just before the end of the season I knocked on the manager's door and told him I'd had enough and asked for my release."

Returning to the North-East in 1969 after three years at Deepdale, Ray began training at Wallsend Sports Centre in the close season. The centre manager was Billy Bell, who offered him the guarantee of a first-team place at Evenwood Town. Before making his decision Ray went to speak to Frank Brennan, the former Newcastle United idol who had led North Shields to victory in the FA Amateur Cup the previous season, but in spite of his experience as an apprentice professional at Preston, the best Brennan was willing to offer him was a starting place in the reserves, so he opted for Evenwood:

"I was still only 18 but I was full of confidence and I was physically strong; I weighed twelve and a half stones. I went there as a centre-forward to play with the likes of Eddie Ross, Colin Hallimond, Tony Monkhouse and Bob Tookey. They were fearsome — as hard as nails. Alex Peters was another good player, and if I got kicked they protected me. They were all lovely people at Evenwood; they never treated me as a townie — I was accepted from the start. We would train on the field in 18 inches of snow and we weren't bothered. Sometimes when you walked across the pitch your hair was frosted! Billy Bell used to pick me up every Monday and Wednesday and take me through for training. We would be sitting in the back of his car talking and Billy would turn round to listen while the car was doing 70 miles an hour in third gear."

Ray (second left, back row) and his big pal Alan Young (fifth left, back row)
at the Wallsend Engineers Club, to receive their trophies

The spirit and commitment engendered by Billy Bell produced spectacular results. In the three seasons Ray Young was at Evenwood they twice won the Northern League championship and his goalscoring prowess and all-round playing ability made him a firm favourite with the crowd. In his first two seasons he scored 29 and 27 goals respectively. Ray's commitment to the club was total: once he had made his decision to play for them, the travelling distance and the inconvenience involved became irrelevant:

"It didn't matter that it was a long way away. I had made the commitment so it wasn't an issue. When you win things it's because you play as a team; you have to have respect for each other. Winning those Northern League titles was nice but it wasn't as important to me as it was to other people. I just wanted to enjoy playing. I was never one to win at all costs, I was happy to play at a good standard. I've always gone to teams for the people — and the social side."

The significance of the 'social side' is difficult to underestimate. By his own admission Ray was now a ten-pints-a-night man, enjoying several pints or so in the clubhouse after training and then adjourning to Durham City centre for further refreshment in the Pot and Glass.

Ray stayed at Evenwood for three happy years but he was also keen to play with his drinking mates on Sunday mornings; this was the reason he resisted all of Evenwood's overtures to sign a contract, because it would have committed him to training on Sundays, when he took the view that the Sunday morning people worked just as hard, and besides he had once again made a commitment. The team in question was Wallsend Engineers, run by Freddie Newton:

"They were a tremendous side. I couldn't always get a game and neither could my best mate Alan Young. People thought we were brothers — some still do. Anyway, with players of the quality of Peter Davidson, Kenny Duffell, Tony Cassidy and John Hamilton around you weren't guaranteed a place. The social side was fantastic, not just on Sundays but on Saturdays as well when we would rush back from playing to get to the Engineers Club for five o'clock. I would put my bag behind the counter and go on the drink. Other teams used to meet there and the atmosphere was great; then we'd go upstairs and by half past ten we would have a lot of drink on board, then go clubbing. We would come back at two in the morning or go on to a party, then play for the Engineers at half past ten the next morning!"

That approach to the game inevitably produced incidents and characters, one such being Willie Tubman, who was thought to be late on one occasion and Freddie Newton wouldn't pick the team without him. Everyone was sitting around reading the Sunday papers and when one of them put his paper down it became apparent that Willie had been there all the time, but he hadn't been recognised because he was wearing a wig he had bought since the last game. There was a cup final replay at the CWS ground in Cowgate, and Ray and Alan Young had been on their customary drinking spree the previous night, going on to separate parties where they had stayed overnight:

"I had my bag which had my kit in as well as a bottle of vodka and a bottle of gin for full-time.

When Alan arrived he asked me where his boots were; he'd been to another party and he thought I had them, but I didn't. He had to borrow a pair of boots but it didn't matter. We were 2-0 up at half-time so we started drinking vodka and orange. We won 4-0 and started on the gin at full-time! Another time we had gone out on the Saturday night after a game and finished up having races between lamp-posts at five o'clock in the morning. Once two of us stripped off and ran around Sunholme Estate naked in the middle of the night."

After eight years at Wallsend Engineers Ray moved to another of the town's social club sides, Wallsend Buffs, where John Montgomery was the manager and Ray and his pals continued to combine Sunday morning football with Saturday night antics. Along with John Montgomery, Howard Trotter, Steve Avery, Frankie Blaine and Jonas Hackworth, Ray would be out on the town along with the assorted wives and girlfriends of the players. The routine usually involved buying cans and bottles of drinks at last orders and going on to someone's house until five in the morning. It was possible to sustain footballing success while indulging in this lifestyle for one reason only: they were brilliant players:

"We were exceptional but I have to admit that sometimes the drink affected even our performances. We sometimes lost games because of it, but no team could match us drinking-wise."

It was quite fashionable in the 1970s for local football teams to organise short trips abroad, usually at the end of the season, and Wallsend Buffs were no exception. Their destination was Benidorm and as may be imagined a good time was had by all:

"The fun started on the plane. Steve Avery and

I were running domino cards and the pilot was calling out the winning numbers. On the Saturday morning Steve and I went to a local bar we called the 'Johnny Mathis Bar' for breakfast. It was quarter to nine so I asked Steve what he fancied. He couldn't make his mind up so we decided to have a half of lager while he thought about it. We were still there at five o'clock in the afternoon and he still hadn't decided."

The return flight from Benidorm to Newcastle was delayed, providing another opportunity to sit around the pool drinking, but one of the players, Howard Trotter, rose above the general level of self-indulgence and went into town to buy a present for his wife, returning with a tasteful leather handbag:

Ray with Lyn Young — and fried rice!

"We thought we should do the same so we sent him back to the shop to buy eleven more, which was great until we all went out together with our wives on the following Saturday night and they all turned up with identical new handbags. They called us some choice names. The only thing I had to eat during those four days in Spain was one Spanish omelette. We got back to Newcastle at half past seven at night so naturally I went to the club. Unfortunately my wife found out what time we had got back so she wouldn't come to pick me up at closing time. To make matters worse she had cooked me a steak and I couldn't eat it; the dog got it. I have to admit I drank a lot but I trained like a demon and I was lucky to avoid serious injury, so I had a good career."

Meanwhile, Ray's Saturday career continued to prosper. After three seasons at Evenwood he joined Blyth Spartans, where he played up-front with Alan Young in a side which reached the quarter-finals of the FA Amateur Cup before going out to Slough Town:

"We thought we were good enough to win the Amateur Cup. Alan and I had a great

Marden over-40's team

understanding and made loads of goals for each other and it was disappointing when we lost to Slough."

A successful spell at South Shields followed, under the management of Bobby Elwell. Ray had a high regard for Elwell and played two predictably eventful seasons for him. His pal and drinking companion at Shields was a solicitor called Lyn Rutherford, a man Ray describes as loving dogs, horses and drink. One Friday night the two of them went on a drinking spree in a pub in Whitley Bay and next day they were picked up to play at Wallington in Northumberland. The excesses of the previous night had a significant influence on their first-half performances, and Bobby Elwell read the riot act at half-time to such sobering effect that they turned a 0-2 midway deficit into a 3-2 victory:

"Rutherford and I were serious. We were always late. We got held up in the Tyne Tunnel this day but Elwell didn't believe us because of our track record so he dropped us. We had some outstanding players at Shields; Billy Graham, Steve Hunter, Kenny Parker. We were due to play at Seaham one Saturday and it was windy as hell. We got the bus down but when the referee put the ball on the centre spot to start the game it blew away. The game was called off so we were in the pub by four o'clock"

Despite indulgences of this kind Ray was part of a South Shields team which achieved a good measure of success, winning the Northern Alliance and Wearside leagues as well as having a good run in the FA Vase. Their demise in the Vase came at the hands of Leicester Old Boys, and Ray believes it was principally as a consequence of bad planning which saw them travel on the day of the match rather than the day before. The journey was a nightmare and the team arrived at their opponents' ground just half an hour before kick off; hardly the ideal preparation for a game they could and should have won, but lost because their preparation wasn't sufficiently professional.

The nucleus of the South Shields team then followed Bobby Elwell to Bishop Auckland, where Ray had a very enjoyable time playing among people he liked in a set-up he regarded as highly professional. The following years saw him on the move on a regular basis; a spell back at South Shields, then a return to Blyth to play for Jackie Marks before spending a season with Newcastle Blue Star. Then came a season at Wallsend before a two-and-a-half-year finale at North Shields:

"1982 was a great season at North Shields under Peter Flaherty. We beat Halifax Town in the first round of the FA Cup and played Walsall in the second round, but by now I was 34 and I was content to spend the next six years just turning out for pleasure for Wallsend Coronation."

When he reached his fortieth birthday Ray began a new career playing in the Over-40s league for Marden under the guidance of his old team-mate Tony Cassidy:

"That's another set of great people; Keith Miller, Alan Chapman, Norman Parfitt, Richard Percy, Jim McFarlane and Tom Sword along with John Weir and John Irwin on the committee. I can honestly say the outstanding highlight of my playing career was being voted player of the year in the Over-40s. It was recognition by people you respect."

Ray Young's outstanding talent as a footballer and a drinker have combined to make his one of the more colourful careers in non-league football. He has been a richly gifted player with a refreshing attitude to the game and a clutch of old-fashioned values like loyalty and commitment. Spare a thought, though, for his wife of 23 years, Lynne. He calls her Lynne Young and fried rice and it says a great deal about her that their relationship has been solid throughout Ray's twin careers as player and drinker. Perhaps like most relationships, it's the little things that have made it work, like a handbag from Benidorm!